Best Easy [

Best Easy Day Hikes
Columbus

Susan Finch

FALCONGUIDES

GUILFORD, CONNECTICUT
HELENA, MONTANA
AN IMPRINT OF THE GLOBE PEQUOT PRESS

FALCONGUIDES®

Copyright © 2009 by Morris Book Publishing, LLC

Falcon, FalconGuides, and Outfit Your Mind are registered trademarks of Morris
Book Publishing, LLC.

TOPO! Explorer software and SuperQuad source maps courtesy of National
Geographic Maps. For information about TOPO! Explorer, TOPO!, and Nat Geo
Maps products, go to www.topo.com or www.natgeomaps.com.

Maps created by Off Route Inc. Copyright Morris Book Publishing, LLC.

Library of Congress Cataloging-in-Publication Data is available on file.

ISBN 978-0-7627-5435-9

Printed in the United States of America

10 9 8 7 6 5 4 3 2 1

Contents

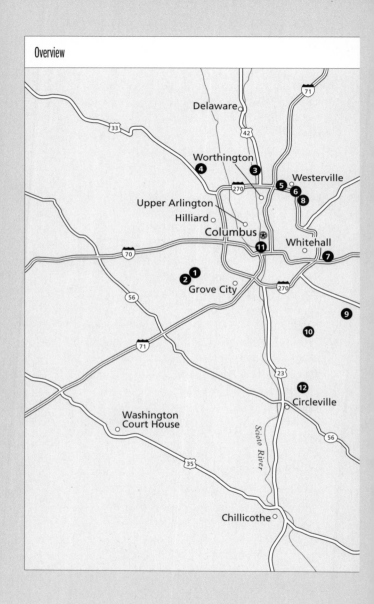

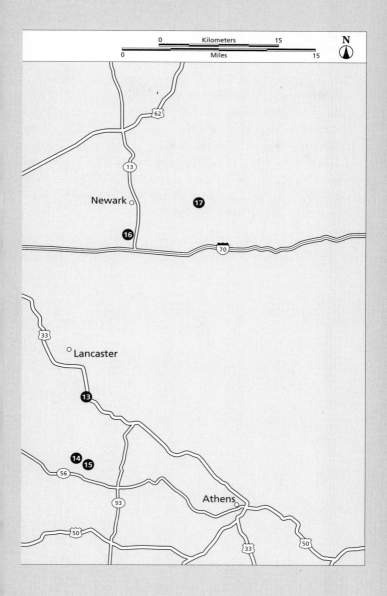

Acknowledgments

Thanks to my best friend, hiking partner, and husband, Drew Padrutt, for all his help and faith in my ability while maneuvering through these hikes. I also want to extend my gratitude to Ron Finch for his unmatched map and hiking insight and Jeannie Finch for all her support and keeping me on task. Also a big thanks to Julie Hill, Columbus Metro Parks, the Ohio State Preserve system, all the park naturalists, and the staff at FalconGuides who shared their vast knowledge and expertise for this book.

Introduction

This guide describes seventeen easy day hikes in the Columbus metro area. Most trails are part of the Columbus metro parks system. Others lie in surrounding central and southeast Ohio, including Circleville, Newark, and the Hocking Hills. Wetland preserves, dense forests, rim trails, jagged outcroppings of blackhand sandstone, elaborate gardens, swamp forests, and gorge trails can all be found in the greater Columbus area.

With year-round access to the metro parks and Ohio preserves, trails may be crowded in summer, during special park programs, and with hike groups in the midst of winter.

Weather

Prepare for snow and ice late November through early March, with temperatures hovering in the teens and below. Averages usually remain in the mid 30s. However, it's not uncommon for the temperature to reach as high as 40 and above on a sunny day. While guided winter hikes are popular at Columbus's metro parks and preserves, boots with adequate traction and warm clothing should be worn. An extra pair of dry socks and gloves is also a good idea.

Springtime in Columbus brings temperatures in the high 50s to 70s, with occasional dips of cool evenings in the mid 30s to 40s. Fall shares similar temperatures with spring, while summer brings comfortably warm days in the mid 70s to 80s, with occasional peaks to the 90s.

The mild variations of weather make hiking in Columbus accessible nearly year-round, although late spring through fall is your best bet for temperate climate and such rewards as colorful wildflowers and brilliant fall foliage.

Zero Impact

Trails in the Columbus area and neighboring parks and preserves are heavily used year-round. We, as trail users and advocates, must be especially vigilant to make sure our passage leaves no lasting mark. Here are some basic guidelines for preserving trails in the region:

- Pack out all your own trash, including biodegradable items like orange peels. You might also pack out garbage left by less-considerate hikers.
- Don't approach or feed any wild creatures—the ground squirrel eyeing your snack food is best able to survive if it remains self-reliant.
- Don't pick wildflowers or gather rocks, antlers, feathers, and other treasures along the trail. Removing these items will only take away from the next hiker's experience.
- Avoid damaging trailside soils and plants by remaining on the established route. This is also a good rule of thumb for avoiding poison ivy, a common regional trailside irritant.
- Don't cut switchbacks, which can promote erosion.
- Be courteous by not making loud noises while hiking.
- Many of these trails are multiuse, which means you'll share them with other hikers, trail runners, mountain bikers, and equestrians. Familiarize yourself with the proper trail etiquette, yielding the trail when appropriate.
- Use outhouses at trailheads or along the trail.

Hiking Safety

Keep the following tips in mind when hiking in the Columbus area:

- Avoid hiking alone or out to isolated rocks, overlooks, swampy terrain, and outcroppings.

- Remember that many of the metro parks and preserves close around sunset. Note the time in advance, and make sure you return to your car in plenty of time.

- Wear boots with adequate traction on your hikes, especially in the rocky region of Hocking Hills. Although the parks are open in winter, rocks can be slippery with ice and difficult to maneuver.

- Stay on marked trails at all times. Many of the listed parks in this book feature protected wetlands and also rope off areas considered dangerous. Always read the park signs and regulations before hiking and exercise caution on all trails, especially elevated rim hikes.

Wilderness Restrictions and Regulations

Columbus metro parks and Ohio state preserves are generally open year-round during daylight hours, but winter and holidays hours may vary. Admission to the parks in this guide is free. Check the Metro Parks Web site at www.metroparks.net or Ohio State Parks at www.ohiodnr.com/parks. Individual park Web sites are provided for each hike in this guide.

How to Use This Guide

This guide is designed to be simple and easy to use. Each hike is described with a map and summary information that delivers the trail's vital statistics, including distance, approximate hiking time, difficulty, trail surface, best season, other trail users, canine compatibility, park schedule, sources for additional maps, and trail contacts.

Directions to the trailhead are also provided, along with a general description of what you'll see along the way. A detailed route finder (Miles and Directions) sets forth mileages between significant landmarks along the trail.

Trail Finder

Best Hikes for River Lovers

1   Indian Ridge and Terrace Trails (Battelle Darby Creek Metro Park)

2   Dyer Mill Trail (Battelle Darby Creek Metro Park)

11   North Bank Park

Best Hikes for Lake Lovers

12   Hargus Lake Trail (A. W. Marion State Park)

16   Dawes Arboretum

Best Hikes for Children

11   North Bank Park (North Bank Park Pavilion to COSI)

10   Kokomo Wetland Trail (Slate Run Metro Park)

16   Dawes Arboretum

Best Hikes for Dogs

4   Marsh Hawk and Ironweed Trails (Glacier Ridge Metro Park)

12   Hargus Lake Trail (A. W. Marion State Park)

15   Old Man's Cave (Hocking Hills State Park)

Best Hikes for Great Views

9   Ridge to Meadows Trail (Chestnut Ridge Metro Park)

14   Rim Trail (Conkle's Hollow State Nature Preserve)

17   Blackhand Gorge Rim Trail (Blackhand Gorge State Nature Preserve)

Best Hikes for Nature Lovers

Best Hikes for History Buffs

Map Legend

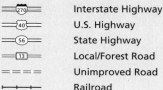	
═══270═══	Interstate Highway
═══40═══	U.S. Highway
═══56═══	State Highway
═══13═══	Local/Forest Road
= = = =	Unimproved Road
├──┼──┼──┤	Railroad
- - - - - - -	Trail
▬▬▬▬▬▬	Featured Route
──────	Paved Trail
⌇⌇⌇	Marsh/Swamp
‿	Bridge
⚠	Campground
❷	Information
₱	Parking
▲	Peak
🛆	Picnic Area
■	Point of Interest
🛈	Ranger Station
🚻	Restroom
⟲	Spring
○	Town
❻	Trailhead
⬢	Viewpoint
⟫	Waterfall

1 Battelle Darby Creek Metro Park: Indian Ridge and Terrace Trails

Hike your way from flat, easy terrain to sloping forest woodlands and get a taste for what the region's largest metro park has to offer.

Distance: 3.8-mile lollipop
Approximate hiking time: 2.5 hours
Difficulty: Moderate due to steep hills
Trail surface: Gravel and dirt
Best season: April through November
Other trail users: None
Canine compatibility: Leashed dogs permitted only on separate

Wagtail Trail
Schedule: Open 6:30 a.m. to 10:00 p.m. April through September; 6:30 a.m. to 8:00 p.m. October through March
Maps: USGS Galloway
Trail contacts: Columbus Metro Parks, 1775 Darby Creek Drive, Galloway, OH 43119; (614) 878-3711; http://metroparks.net/ParksBattelleDarbyCreek.aspx

Finding the trailhead: From Interstate 270 take the U.S. Highway 40/West Broad Street exit going west. Continue for 5 miles on Broad Street and turn left onto Darby Creek Drive. The main entrance is located approximately 3 miles on the right. Park at the Cedar Ridge Picnic Area. GPS coordinates: N53 59.89' / W83 12.67'

The Hike

The largest park in the system, Battelle Darby Creek Metro Park features 6,786 acres of rolling fields, forests, and open prairies with 11 miles of trails ranging from easy to difficult. Hikers can choose from a selection of secluded walks, popular footpaths, guided hikes, and dog-friendly multipurpose trails.

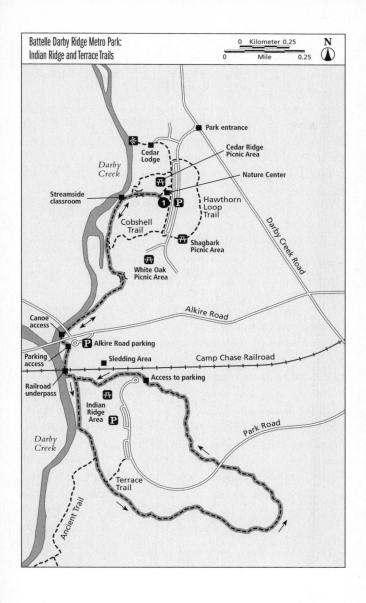

Battelle Darby Ridge Metro Park:
Indian Ridge and Terrace Trails

0   Kilometer   0.25

0   Mile   0.25

N

Park entrance

Cedar Ridge
Picnic Area

Nature Center

Cedar Lodge

Darby
Creek

Hawthorn
Loop
Trail

Streamside
classroom

1

P

Darby Creek Road

Cobshell
Trail

Shagbark
Picnic Area

White Oak
Picnic Area

Alkire Road

Canoe
access

Alkire Road parking

Parking
access

Sledding Area

Camp Chase Railroad

Railroad
underpass

Access to parking

Indian
Ridge
Area

P

Park Road

Darby
Creek

Ancient Trail

Terrace
Trail

The park is also popular for its ongoing efforts to preserve local rivers and wildlife. The Indian Ridge to Terrace Trail hike features Big and Little Darby Creeks, designated as both state and national scenic rivers and home to more than one hundred species of fish and invertebrates, including Ohio's endangered mussels. In 2004 *The Columbus Dispatch* reported that Big Darby was named one of the Most Endangered Rivers in the United States. Organizations work throughout the year in support of ongoing efforts to protect the delicate ecosystem.

In addition to learning more about Ohio's endangered species, hikers can enjoy spectacular views of the river throughout the park and get lost in a forest of buckeye, sycamore, silver maple, and box elder. The southern portion of the trail is home to shagbark hickories; red, gray, fox, and flying squirrels; and chipmunks.

The park also has no shortage of colorful wildflowers scattered throughout the park. Slopes and bluffs along the stream feature purple coneflower, prairie false indigo, and Indian paintbrush. Attentive hikers might be able to spot goldenseal and drooping trillium nestled along the hills.

For an expansive sampling of what the park and rivers have to offer at Battelle Darby, start your hike at the Cobshell trailhead and wind your way through the Indian Ridge and Terrace Trails. The Cobshell hike includes moderate terrain due to steep stairs at the start of this trail section and rolling hills leading out to Indian Ridge. Starting with Cobshell allows hikers to follow along Darby Creek and switch from moderate to easy to terrain and back again. There's also ample opportunity for both a leisurely and challenging hike along the way, with options for additional trails.

Start your hike at the Cobshell trailhead, located in the parking lot to the left of the Nature Center. While you're there, pick up a trail map or ask one of the park's naturalists for a little insight into the local wildlife and fauna before heading out. Park naturalists can also offer more information about the history of the area, including the park's Adena mound located off Ancient Trail. You can also inquire about ongoing educational programs and group hikes offered year-round.

Following the gravel path, hike down the steep wooden and gravel stairs and cross a bridge for a view of Big Darby Creek. It's a vivid introduction to what the hike will offer in terms of alternating stream life and tranquil woodlands. You'll also discover several opportunities for up-close vantage points to the banks of Big and Little Darby Creeks.

At 0.3 mile cross a short wooden bridge and wind your way uphill. From here you'll cross another wooden bridge and hike into the forest. Listen for the abundance of gray tree frogs in the area, which are loudest during early spring. If you look along the trail, you might see small amphibian pools created by the metro parks system. Although relatively new, they already show signs of use. Indian Ridge Trail is heavily wooded with a thick canopy cover until it takes a surprising bend out of the woods and goes underneath several overpasses.

At 0.7 mile walk under the first overpass and take note of the creek and the collection of large stones lining the banks. The area is an ideal rest stop for a picnic or photo opportunity at the water's edge.

Walk under two more overpasses, the last being a railroad trestle. If you're hiking during spring or fall, you might hear an occasional train going to and back from the village of Lilly Chapel, just a couple miles to the west. This seasonal train runs grain and seed to and from the town's granary.

When you reach a trail fork at 0.9 mile, bear right to continue onto the Terrace Trail. Your hike will eventually loop back to this point.

The beginning of Terrace Trail is relatively open and less wooded than Cobshell to Indian Ridge. You should pass open fields on your left, with trees lining the trail. At 1.2 miles a fork leads right for Ancient Trail. This area of Battelle Darby features a ceremonial Adena mound, which is not uncommon in the metro parks system. At dusk this stretch is especially beautiful when fireflies flock to the area and dazzle visitors.

To continue your hike from the Ancient Trail fork, keep straight and continue the loop back to Indian Ridge. From here Terrace Trail alternates from flat and easy terrain to sloping hills. Keep winding through a dense canopy of woods and fallen logs, ideal for bird and wildlife viewing. This section of the park also includes a swamp forest and is the most secluded area of the hike. At 2.2 miles cross the road and make your way past a parking lot and picnic area complete with restrooms; bear right to continue. Keep hiking until you reach the beginning of your loop at the Indian Ridge–Terrace Trail fork at 2.9 miles.

To visit the Adena mound, bear left to make your way back to Ancient Trail. Otherwise, backtrack to the Cobshell trailhead and nature center.

Miles and Directions

0.0 Start at the Cobshell trailhead to the left of the Nature Center.

0.3 Cross a short wooden bridge; walk uphill and continue walking west.

0.4 Cross another wooden bridge and continue straight as the trail slopes uphill through the forest.

0.7 Walk under the first overpass and next to large stones on the creek banks.

0.9 Bear right at a trail fork to continue onto Terrace Trail.

1.2 The fork to the right leads to Ancient Trail. Keep straight.

2.2 Cross the road and make your way past a parking lot and picnic area with restrooms, bearing right.

2.9 Reach the end of the loop of Indian Ridge-Terrace Trail. Bear right to return to the trailhead. (Option: Turn left and backtrack to Ancient Trail to view the Adena mound.)

3.8 Arrive back at the trailhead and nature center.

2 Battelle Darby Creek Metro Park: Dyer Mill Trail

Leave the city behind and get lost in nature on this 2.5-mile hike. Follow along Little Darby Creek and loop into tall grass meadows and secluded woodlands. Hikers will get a taste of scenic river views, wildlife spotting, and open, tranquil fields.

Distance: 2.5-mile loop

Approximate hiking time: 1.5 hours

Difficulty: Moderate due to hills

Trail surface: Grass and gravel

Best season: April through November and after a snowfall

Other trail users: Hikers and cross-country skiers

Canine compatibility: Leashed dogs permitted only on separate Wagtail Trail

Schedule: Open 6:30 a.m. to 10:00 p.m. April through September; 6:30 a.m. to 8:00 p.m. October through March

Maps: USGS Galloway

Trail contacts: Columbus Metro Parks, 1775 Darby Creek Drive, Galloway, OH 43119; (614) 878-3711; http://metroparks .net/ParksBattelleDarbyCreek .aspx

Finding the trailhead: Take Interstate 270 to the U.S. Highway 40/West Broad Street exit going west. Drive for 5 miles on Broad Street and turn left onto Darby Creek Drive. Drive 3 miles and pass the park's Cedar Ridge entrance. Turn right onto Alkire Road and right again onto Gardner Road. Park near the seasonal ice-skating pond. (This entrance is 1.4 miles from the Battelle Darby Cedar Ridge park entrance.) The trailhead is marked with a large sign at the end of the parking lot near the park entrance. GPS coordinates: N53 41.40' / W83 13.25'

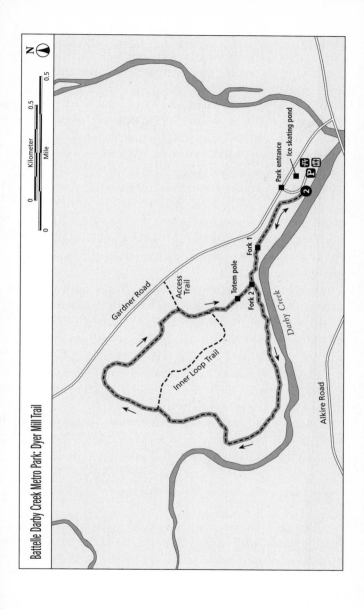

Battelle Darby Creek Metro Park: Dyer Mill Trail

The Hike

The Dyer Mill Trail is part of Battelle Darby Metro Park, the largest in the system. Dubbed one of the "last Great Places in the Western Hemisphere" by The Nature Conservancy, the park boasts oak-hickory forests, open meadows, a diverse ecosystem, and stunning views over Little and Big Darby Creeks. Frequent educational programs, festivities, group activities, winter hikes, and night hikes are scheduled year-round through the nature center.

Although you won't be able to see the remains, the parking lot and lowland areas near the borders of the Dyer Mill Trail were once used as a baseball field. Before that, the area was home to a gristmill that served the local community for decades.

Unlike many of the other hikes in the metro parks system, Dyer Mill encompasses a wooded nature trail and a winter ski trail. The trail alternates between grass trails, meadows, and wooded forests with towering sugar maple and oak trees. Winter lines the branches with ice and powder after a fresh snowfall. Fall is an especially beautiful time to visit and watch the leaves change. You'll also discover bright leaf litter peppering the trail.

Hiking Dyer Mill tends to be a solitary experience; you'll rarely cross paths with other hikers. Before the leaves turn and the trees go bare, it's easy to feel positively isolated. However, in winter this trail can receive heavy traffic from cross-country skiers, as well as visitors looking for prime spots to sled.

Regardless of the season, this 2.5-mile hike features open grassland with easy terrain for hikers of all ages. Start by finding the trailhead sign at the southwest end of the parking lot. You'll notice a seasonal ice-skating pond on your right as you walk to the trailhead. Walk along the grassy path until you hit the gravel and dirt portion of the trail. There are many small forks splintering right throughout the hike, so make sure to keep bearing left to stay on the main trail.

At 0.3 mile you'll reach the end of the entry trail and a fork. You can go either right or left, but for this hike bear left. Head down a steep hill and level off alongside Little Darby Creek. This is the best area for active wildlife viewing. While taking a moment to enjoy the creek, listen for birds quarreling over a midmorning snack.

Big and Little Darby Creeks are full of endangered fish and invertebrates, including several mussels and other mollusks. The national conservation group American Rivers named it Big Darby. The immediate threat comes from encroaching urbanization. The park system and private organizations are working year-round to preserve the area's unique ecosystem and aquatic life.

While the Dyer Mill Trail doesn't include a variety of scenic waypoints and stops along the way, it does offer a chance to spend a few hours relatively lost in nature. Visitors can sample one of the best spots for hiking, cross-country skiing, and wildlife viewing. As you wind into the open meadows and tall grass, you'll notice wooden bird boxes peppering the area as well as activity from the drier ridges above the creek. Redheaded woodpecker, magnolia warbler, ruby-crowned kinglet, and scarlet tanager are just some of the birds you might see. If you have a pair of binoculars, stop along the grasslands or at the ridge to get a better view.

During your hike you'll notice several forks splintering along the main trail that lead to an outer loop. Accessing this trail will extend your total hike to 3.2 miles. For this hike, keep following the well-posted nature trail signs or wooden posts marked with blue hiker emblems.

While walking through the open prairies, look for large birds of prey. Park naturalist Tim Taylor noted that there is almost always a red-tailed hawk nesting along the perimeter of the field. During summer, colorful butterflies can be found floating past the tall grasses.

Walk through the open meadows and wind back into the woods. Continue to bear left until you reach the end of the loop. Turn left and backtrack to the trailhead off the parking lot.

Miles and Directions

0.0 Start at the trailhead, located off the parking lot past the ice-skating pond.

0.3 Reach the entry trail at the beginning of the loop. Bear left, walking downhill along Little Darby Creek.

0.7 Continue following along Little Darby Creek through the woods.

1.0 Continue on the loop, bearing left and staying on the main trail.

2.2 Reach the end of the loop; turn left onto the entry trail.

2.5 Arrive back at the trailhead.

3 Highbanks Metro Park: Overlook and Dripping Rock Trails

Wind through Edward F. Hutchins State Nature Preserve and stop by the observation deck for a 110-foot-elevation view of the Olentangy River. Meet up with Dripping Rock Trail for a hike through hardwood forests and shale outcroppings to see why this area has been designated a National Natural Landmark.

Distance: 4.1-mile double loop

Approximate hiking time: 2.5 to 3 hours

Difficulty: Moderate due to length and some hills

Trail surface: Paved and gravel

Best season: March through November

Other trail users: Joggers

Canine compatibility: Leashed dogs permitted only on separate Coyote Run, Big Meadows, and Oak Coves Path

Schedule: Open 6:30 a.m. to 10:00 p.m. April through September; 6:30 a.m. to 8:00 p.m. October through March

Maps: USGS Powell

Trail contacts: Columbus Metro Parks, 9466 Columbus Pike (U.S. Highway 23 North), Lewis Center, OH 43035; (614) 846-9962; http://metroparks.net/ParksHighbanks.aspx

Finding the trailhead: From Interstate 270 take US 23 N. Drive for 3 miles and look for the main park entrance on the left. If you hit Powell Road, you've gone too far. Park at the Oak Coves Picnic Area. GPS coordinates: N8 54.99' / W83 01.88'

The Hike

Highbanks Metro Park is a reminder of Ohio's rich topo–

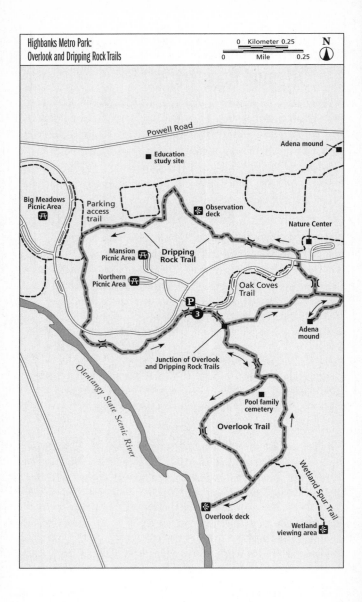

Highbanks Metro Park:
Overlook and Dripping Rock Trails

0   Kilometer   0.25

0   Mile   0.25

N

Powell Road

Adena mound

Education
study site

Big Meadows
Picnic Area

Parking
access
trail

Observation
deck

Nature Center

Mansion
Picnic Area

Dripping
Rock Trail

Northern
Picnic Area

Oak Coves
Trail

P
3

Adena
mound

Junction of Overlook
and Dripping Rock Trails

Olentangy State Scenic River

Pool family
cemetery

Overlook Trail

Wetland Spur Trail

Overlook deck

Wetland
viewing area

graphical diversity, Native American heritage, and pre-historic influence. Exposed shale bluffs, deep ravines, and ancient Adena burial mounds comingle with oak-hickory, beech-maple, and floodplain hardwood forests. Staff at the park's nature center can tell you more about the shale banks and their protruding, bowling ball–shaped rocks that formed out of organic materials during the Devonian period. The nature center also has prime window views to watch the nearly sixty species of birds that live in the area, including finches and woodpeckers.

Highbanks boasts a spectacular hike with historical way-points and contrasting landscapes between its high bluffs and ravines. Start your hike at the trailhead adjacent to the Oak Coves Picnic Area near the map kiosk. Head downhill along the gravel trail. At 0.1 mile walk over a wooden bridge and continue uphill before reaching the fork for Dripping Rock and Overlook Trails. The path is wide and dotted with wooden fences that remind hikers and joggers to stay on the trail.

Continue straight, following the signs for Overlook Trail, and pass the Pool family cemetery. The cemetery was originally established in the 1800s. Park personnel discovered the stacked gravestones on the land in the 1980s and moved them to their present location. The Pools are thought to have been the area's first white inhabitants.

The entire loop is a popular running haunt, especially on weekends. Keep an eye out for passing joggers, and stay to one side of the trail. As you walk onward past the cemetery, note the 1,500-foot earthwork shaped like an oversize C, or a horseshoe. A nearby sign explains that the earthwork was likely the fortification for an ancient village constructed by the Cole Indians for protection. This area has been designated a National Natural Landmark and is continuously being studied by geologists, nature enthusiasts, and students from area universities.

Keep following signs toward the overlook deck for stunning views of the Olentangy River, complete with towering shale banks and looming sycamore trees below the overlook deck. This 110-foot-high area also features benches and is an ideal place to take a break to enjoy the scenery. It won't be difficult to see why the Olentangy has been designated an Official Scenic River by the state of Ohio for its mostly undisturbed condition and overall beauty. Except for ongoing development and new construction dotting Route 315 across the water, this stop is a tranquil escape.

Backtrack and continue straight along Overlook Trail while noticing some of the wildlife and surrounding trees. American beech, maples, white ash, wild black cherry, and bush honeysuckle thrive along the trail and in the ravines. Red-bellied woodpeckers pick at dead trees, while tufted titmice and cardinals forage for food.

At 1.3 miles you can bear right for the Wetland Spur Trail to view migrating geese and ducks from a bird blind overlooking a pond or continue straight to make your way back to the fork of Overlook and Dripping Rock Trails. For this hike, from the fork continue straight on Dripping Rock Trail and follow along the streams and tributaries that drain off the Olentangy. You'll discover a variety of spiny honey locust trees and more intimate views of the shale bluffs that contrast against the deep ravines.

Continue past the fork for the spur trail leading to an ancient Adena mound. At 2.9 miles look for wild black cherry trees and open fields with an observation deck. In spring you might come across yellow trout lilies and other colorful wildflowers. At 3.6 miles walk under a low underpass and bear left. Make your way uphill before crossing a creek on a wooden bridge. Keep following along the wooden reminder fences and cross a final bridge at 4.0 miles. Pass through the parking lot to return to the trailhead.

Miles and Directions

0.0 Start at the trailhead adjacent to the Oak Coves Picnic Area.

0.1 Walk over a wooden bridge and continue uphill to find the fork for Dripping Rock and Overlook Trails. Stay straight to continue on the Overlook Trail.

0.9 Turn right and walk down to observation deck. Afterwards, backtrack to the intersection and continue straight.

1.3 At the fork continue straight to the junction of Overlook and Dripping Rock Trails. (Option: Bear right onto the Wetland Spur Trail to visit the bird blind.)

2.3 Pass spur trail to the Adena mound.

2.9 Stop at the observation deck over open fields.

3.6 Walk under a low underpass and bear left; walk uphill and cross a creek on a wooden bridge.

4.0 Cross a final bridge.

4.1 Walk through the parking lot to arrive back at the trailhead.

4 Glacier Ridge Metro Park: Marsh Hawk and Ironweed Trails

Now surrounded by farmlands, Glacier Ridge was named for the moraine that was left by the retreating Wisconsinan glacier. Today the area features a restored 250-acre wetland, a boardwalk, and an observation tower for a leisurely and informative hike.

Distance: 3.2-mile shuttle or 6.4 miles out and back

Approximate hiking time: 2 hours one way and 4 hours out and back

Difficulty: Easy

Trail surface: Paved

Best season: April through October

Other trail users: Bicyclists

Canine compatibility: Leashed dogs permitted

Schedule: Open daily 6:30 a.m. to dark

Maps: USGS Shawnee Hills

Trail contacts: Columbus Metro Parks, 9801 Hyland Croy Road, Plain City, OH 43064; (614) 873-7154; http://metroparks .net/TrailsGlacierRidge.aspx

Finding the trailhead: From Interstate 270 North take exit 17B for U.S. Highway 33/Route 161 west toward Marysville. Follow US 33/Route 161 west to the Route 161/Plain City/Post Road exit. Turn right at the light and then take an immediate left onto Hyland Croy Road. For hikers dropping off a car to pick up at the end of the trail, the Honda Wetland Education Area is 1 mile north on the left at 7825 Hyland Croy Road. To reach the park's main entrance, drive 2 miles farther north and take a left at the roundabout, opposite Glacier Ridge Elementary School. Park by the disc golf course. GPS coordinates: N9 16.09' / W83 11.60'

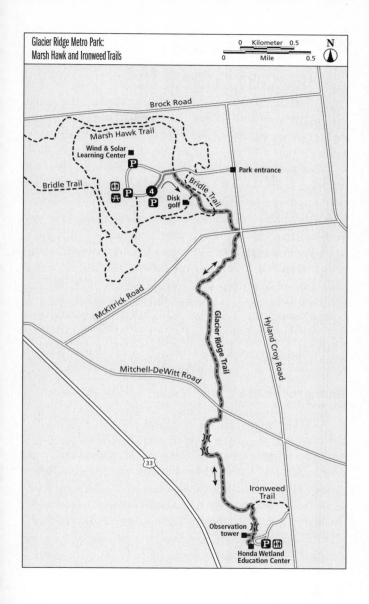

Glacier Ridge Metro Park:
Marsh Hawk and Ironweed Trails

0   Kilometer   0.5

0   Mile   0.5

N

Brock Road

Marsh Hawk Trail

Wind & Solar
Learning Center

P

Bridle Trail

P

P

4

P

Disk
golf

Park entrance

Bridle Trail

McKitrick Road

Glacier Ridge Trail

Hyland Croy Road

Mitchell-DeWitt Road

33

Ironweed
Trail

Observation
tower

P

Honda Wetland
Education Center

The Hike

The 1,037-acre Glacier Ridge Metro Park offers multiuse trail options in a condensed area known for its wetland education access and public programs. One of the newer metro parks in the system, Glacier Ridge features agricultural land, woodlots, successional areas, and large open fields.

The paved multi-use trails are both bike and dog friendly. Plastic bags for canine cleanup are available from the wooden kiosks located along Ironweed Trail. A special horse-only trail—the Savannah, or Bridle, Trail—is also open to cross-country skiing when conditions permit.

Your best option to see the park's wildflowers, successional fields, wetlands, and rolling farmlands is to start at the parking lot near the disc golf course entrance and make your way down the paved trail. The Marsh Hawk trailhead is marked only with a sign that says MULTI-USE TRAIL. If you're looking for an easy day hike, team up with a hiking buddy and drop another car at the nearby Honda Wetland Education Center parking lot, where this hike ends. To spend a more challenging day on the trail, backtrack from the education center for a 6.4-mile hike.

From the main parking lot by the disc golf course, walk 0.2 mile. Turn right at another MULTI-USE TRAIL sign to pick up the Ironweed Trail. You'll walk past an equestrian area with a red barn and cross the grassy 5.0-mile Savannah, or Bridle, Trail several times. You should also be able to see the outskirts of the disc golf course. Watch out for "golfers" with flying discs. Continue past a variety of residential homes, barns, and open fields as you make your way through a short stretch of woods.

Glacier Ridge is not known for its forest cover, and fencerows represent most of its wooded vegetation. The park has ongoing plans for intense reforestation of its original oak, maple, beech, and swamp forest. While the hike isn't ideal for those hoping to see lush vegetation or fall color and get lost in nature, it does offer stunning wildflower displays and open fields with bird-watching opportunities. In late summer and early fall, aster, goldenrod, and purple coneflower can be found at the south end of the park.

Cross McKitrick Road at 0.8 mile and make your way down a gradually winding path with tall grass and open fields. From here continue through Glacier Ridge's successional fields of wildflowers and grasses. Take the time to read the signs posted with information about conservation efforts and the park's history. You'll also see a few bird boxes for migrating feathered visitors and year-round residents.

At 2.0 miles cross Mitchell-DeWitt Road and wind right into the fields. In the distance you'll see encroaching developments and residential homes. While urbanization existed before the multiuse trail ever did, the park has made efforts to restore some of its original landscape. For example, the small pools along the hike are actually restored vernal pools. Each pool is approximately 12 to 18 inches wide and has gradual slopes covered in leaf material and muck. The park was originally agricultural land, and Glacier Ridge personnel tested the soil and surveyed the land to determine where to restore its pools and wetlands.

At 2.9 miles continue straight for the paved trail or turn right for a wooden boardwalk that zigzags over the wetlands to the Honda Wetland Education Center. If you have a dog in tow, you'll need to continue along the paved path; dogs are strictly prohibited from the boardwalk.

Wood ducks, blue herons, dragonflies, turtles, and other wildlife call this 200-acre wetland home. To get a better view of what the wetlands have to offer, stop at the small overlook near the end of the boardwalk before continuing on to the gravel path and parking lot.

You've essentially reached the end of the trail. However, you can turn right to climb the observation tower for views of the Columbus area and a look at what you just hiked. The metal tower has a few winding steps to the top, so it may not be a good option for young children. After visiting the tower, access the paved trail and wind your way to the back of the education center for restrooms, maps, and information resources.

While you're at the education center, take some time to read about the park's ongoing efforts to preserve Ohio's wetlands. Educational programs, available throughout the year, include wildlife tracking, winter survival training, and birding.

If you dropped off a car at the education center, you've completed your hike. Otherwise, retrace your steps to the main park entrance and trailhead.

Miles and Directions

0.0 Start at the paved multi-use trail by the disc golf course.

0.2 Turn right at the MULTI-USE TRAIL sign to pick up the Ironweed Trail.

0.8 Cross McKitrick Road; hike down a gradually winding path with tall grass and open fields.

2.0 Cross Mitchell-DeWitt Road and wind right.

2.9 Continue straight to stay on the paved trail, or turn right to pick up the wooden boardwalk over the wetlands. (FYI: No dogs are permitted on the boardwalk.)

3.2 Arrive at the Honda Wetland Education Center. Unless you've arranged for a shuttle, retrace your steps.

6.4 Arrive back at the trailhead.

5 Sharon Woods Metro Park: Edward S. Thompson and Spring Creek Trails

Hike through 762 acres of open meadows and bur oak forests before taking a stroll alongside Schrock Lake.

Distance: 2.4-mile loop

Approximate hiking time: 1 hour

Difficulty: Moderate due to some hills

Trail surface: Paved and gravel

Best season: April through October

Other trail users: None

Canine compatibility: Dogs not permitted

Schedule: Open 6:30 a.m. to 10:00 p.m. April through September; 6:30 a.m. to 8:00 p.m. October through March

Maps: USGS Northeast Columbus

Trail contacts: Columbus Metro Parks, 6911 Cleveland Avenue, Westerville, OH 43081; (614) 895-6225; http://metroparks .net/ParksSharonWoods.aspx

Finding the trailhead: From Interstate 270 exit at Cleveland Avenue North. Drive 0.5 mile and continue north on Cleveland Avenue and turn left onto Main Street. Turn left into the park entrance at 1.4 miles. Park at the Schrock Lake Picnic Area. GPS coordinates: N6 44.35' / W82 57.72'

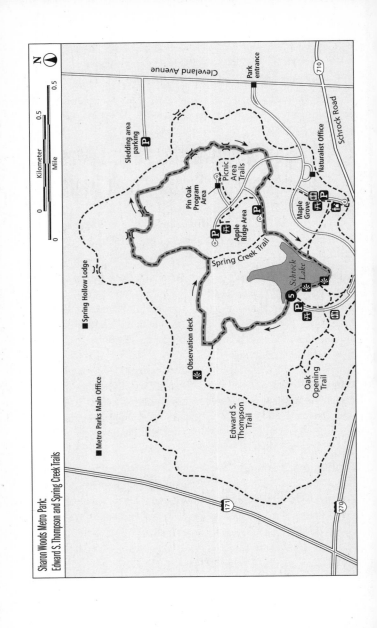

Sharon Woods Metro Park:
Edward S. Thompson and Spring Creek Trails

The Hike

This easy hike through Sharon Woods Metro Park features abundant wetlands and wildlife with an ongoing preservation effort by the metro park system. Despite its hiking opportunities, the park's crowning glory is Schrock Lake.

Walk along the southern region of the park to access the lakeshore, benches, and many picnic areas for a glimpse of the lake's resident bass, crappie, catfish, and bluegill. The lake is also a popular spot for sunbathers. Currently fishing in the lake is permitted for children age fifteen and under and seniors sixty years and older.

Like most of Columbus's metro parks, the nature trails in Sharon Woods do not allow dogs, but a multipurpose paved trail around Sharon Woods is canine compatible. For those accessing the nature trails, this park is home to beech and oak trees, seasonal pools and swamp forest with amphibian habitats, and seasonal breeding grounds.

Park your car next to Schrock Lake for easy access to the Edward S. Thompson Trail. As you're facing the lake, look left to find the trailhead and start your hike on the gravel path. At 0.4 mile continue straight if you want to complete the 1.0-mile Edward S. Thompson Trail. This portion of the trail winds through a 319-acre state nature preserve and features bur oaks and an observation deck for wildlife viewing. For the hike described here, turn right at the fork to access Spring Creek Trail; walk onto the grass path with open fields and tall grass.

While you're hiking through the meadows, you'll notice several bird boxes dotting the landscape. At 0.6 mile look left for a brief spur trail leading to a few bird boxes where you can look for feathered visitors.

The portion of the hike along the meadows is simple and offers little variety. What it does have are vibrant wild-flowers, along with a big-sky effect. On a clear day the sky envelops the tall grass for what seems like miles as you make your way back into the canopied forest. The meadows are lively with goldenrod, New England aster, and bull thistle. Curious goldfinches and clouded sulphur and other butter-flies can be seen flitting through the meadows.

After you hike into the forest, you'll notice a brief over-look area on the left at 1.0 mile with views of the valley and creek formed by a glacier. Follow along the creek as it spiders under bridges and through ravines. This portion of Spring Creek Trail introduces hikers to a handful of steep hills and bursts of short, wooden bridges crossing over the creek.

Keep an eye out for white-tailed deer, and consider the efforts Sharon Woods Metro Park has made to maintain a delicate balance of animal and plant life. In the 1980s and 1990s the deer population grew exponentially after urban-ization around the park. Park personnel began to notice severe plant damage and species loss among the Liliaceae and Orchidaceae plant families. After about 150 plant spe-cies disappeared, the local reptile, bird, invertebrate, and mammal life also dwindled. To restore some of the park's natural habitat, Sharon Woods personnel have worked to control the deer density and manage plant life and vegeta-tion.

Continue hiking through the forest. After a brief reen-try into the meadows, you'll notice a low wooden bridge followed by a woodland pool to your left. Local insect life and bats inhabit the area, and the park displays information about its wildlife on adjacent signs.

From here walk uphill and bear right until you see a parking lot. Bear left and hike past the meadows and parking lots, past the playgrounds and restrooms. At 2.1 miles bear right and start walking alongside Schrock Lake. This area of the park features an urban design with playgrounds, restrooms, picnic pavilions, and various entry points to the benches and information kiosks by the lake. Stop here to enjoy the views before continuing to the parking lot and the hike's end at the Edward S. Thompson trailhead.

Miles and Directions

- **0.0** Start at the trailhead adjacent to Schrock Lake.
- **0.6** Pass a spur trail on the left leading to bird boxes.
- **1.2** Cross a small wooden bridge.
- **1.5** Cross a wooden bridge and walk uphill.
- **2.1** Bear right to continue the trail, and start walking along side Schrock Lake.
- **2.4** Arrive back at Schrock Lake and the trailhead.

6 Inniswood Metro Gardens

Hike through a scenic nature preserve featuring over 2,000 species of plants, a rock garden, flowerbeds, and woodlands.

Distance: 1.4-mile loop
Approximate hiking time: 30 minutes to 1 hour or more, depending on the time you take to enjoy the feature gardens
Difficulty: Easy
Trail surface: Paved and gravel with boardwalk
Best season: March through October
Other trail users: None

Canine compatibility: Leashed dogs permitted on separate Chipmunk Chatter Trail
Schedule: Open daily 7:00 a.m. to dark
Maps: USGS Northeast Columbus
Trail contacts: Columbus Metro Parks, 940 S. Hempstead Road, Westerville, OH 43081; (614) 891-0700; http://metroparks .net/ParksInniswood.aspx

Finding the trailhead: Take Interstate 270 to the Route 3/Westerville Road exit. Go south on Westerville Road to Dempsey Road and turn left. Drive 0.8 mile to Hempstead Road and turn left. Follow Hempstead Road as it jogs right past the Blendon Senior Center. The park entrance is located about 100 yards on your right. Park at the only lot in the park, just off the garden entrance. GPS coordinates: N6 03.35' / W82 53.93'

The Hike

Inniswood Metro Gardens is a 121-acre urban oasis with beautifully cultivated gardens and woodlands. This easy loop hike winds through paved paths, a nature boardwalk, streams, wooded terrain, theme gardens, and of course seasonal flowers.

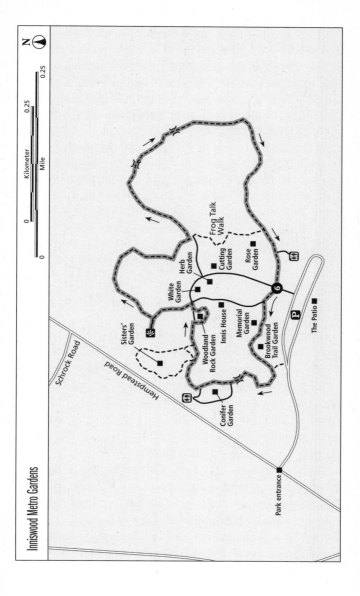

The original grounds were part of Grace and Mary Innis's thirty-seven-acre estate and home. The Innis sisters shared an affinity for gardening and wildlife preservation and donated their property to the metro park system in 1972. Inniswood utilizes its spectacular floral setting and honors the mission of its namesake patrons by encouraging horticulture education and festivities throughout the year. The Innis sisters' former home currently serves as staff offices and a program center.

The result of the sisters' ongoing vision is a tranquil refuge tucked away within its urban boundaries. Inniswood's varied plant collection includes hostas, daffodils, daylilies, and elaborate theme gardens, giving visitors the impression of wandering through a secluded botanical garden. The grounds also possess a fairy-tale quality, with whimsical details including child-size statues, gingerbread-style buildings, and picture-perfect flowerbeds. Its simple paths and flat terrain also make it an easy way to spend the day wandering through the gardens or just make a quick loop through the park.

Inniswood's forks and bends are designed so that you can easily move from one trail to the next, backtrack, and vary your hike according to your time and inclination.

Begin your hike at the front entrance, marked by a pavilion with benches and a map kiosk. Bear left to begin your loop along the paved path. Keep bearing left and walk through the gardens and rolling lawns. At 0.2 mile cross a short stone bridge and bear right at the fork.

Look for the ornate, oversize flower sculptures marking the entrance of the feature garden, called Sisters' Garden. This garden was created to honor Mary and Grace Innis—a tribute to their preservation efforts and public donations. Turn left to explore the small garden, or keep walking straight to continue this hike.

At 0.4 mile turn right to explore the Woodland Rock Garden and wind uphill through the rock-paved path and waterfall area. A short set of stone stairs lead up to rocky crevices and views of the park. Be careful during winter months, when ice makes the area slippery to explore. (Although Inniswood is open year-round, the park tends to close the rock garden and other paths that might ice during winter.)

The trail forks from the exit of the rock garden. Going straight will allow you to explore more of the park's feature gardens. For this hike, turn left to pick up Spring Run Trail. Walk over a bridge and onto the gravel path. Stay on Spring Run until you reach 0.5 mile. Stop and turn left to access an overlook of the woodlands and area wildlife, or turn right to continue the trail.

Spring Creek Trail winds through a forest and over streams and focuses on the park's woodlands. This portion of the hike also retains a special childhood element, with a forest as its setting. Note the charming light-blue picnic gazebo on your right at 0.6 mile before the trail curves left out of the forest and into an open field.

After making your way from the field, you'll hike back into the forest. Turn left at 0.7 mile for the Boardwalk Preserve Trail. The wooden boardwalk takes visitors over bridges, an open field, and gravel paths while offering close-up views of the local wildlife and foliage. Look for deciduous conifers, oak, hickory, beech, and maples along with native wildflowers. This is a good spot to keep an eye out for warblers and pileated woodpeckers, which make themselves at home in the area woodlands.

Although Inniswood is a small park, it offers a surprisingly rich diversity of landscape. As you walk from the paved paths past the stone garden, lawns, statues, wooden

bridges, flowerbeds, and winding woodlands, stop to consider each area's distinctive floral and ornamental value.
Beds of hostas and daylilies and terra-cotta pots strategically
placed throughout the park offer a sense of fluidity from
one section to the next. An herb garden, thyme collection,
and more than a hundred varieties of hardy ferns can also be
found throughout the park.

At 1.3 miles you can turn right to hike the 0.1-mile
Frog Talk Walk Trail or continue straight to the end of this
hike. Look left for the restrooms, or keep walking straight
to access your original trailhead. This is a good time to turn
right and hike a new leg of the park to explore some of the
feature gardens you might have missed on the way. Otherwise turn left and return to the parking lot.

Inniswood's forks and bends are designed so that you
can easily move from one trail to the next, backtrack, and
vary your hike.

Miles and Directions

0.0 Start at the Inniswood front entrance. Bear left to begin the
loop.

0.2 Cross a stone bridge and continue right at the fork.

0.4 Turn right to explore the Woodland Rock Garden and wind
uphill through the rock-paved path.

0.5 Turn right to continue the trail. (Option: Turn left for the
woodlands overlook.)

0.6 Pass a picnic gazebo on your right. The trail curves left out of
the forest and into an open field.

0.7 Turn left onto the Boardwalk Preserve Trail.

1.3 Continue straight at the fork. (Option: Turn right to walk to
the 0.1-mile Frog Talk Walk Trail fork.)

1.4 Arrive back at the trailhead.

7 Blacklick Woods Metro Park

The oldest metro park in the system, this 643–acre park features relatively undisturbed forest and wildlife with open meadows, fields, and seasonal ponds.

Distance: 1.9-mile loop
Approximate hiking time: 1.5 hours
Difficulty: Easy
Trail surface: Gravel
Best season: March through November
Other trail users: None
Canine compatibility: Dogs not permitted

Schedule: Open 6:30 a.m. to 10:00 p.m. April through September; 6:30 a.m. to 8:00 p.m. October through March
Maps: USGS Reynoldsburg
Trail contacts: Columbus Metro Parks, 6975 E. Livingston Ave., Reynoldsburg, OH 43068; (614) 861-8759; http://metroparks .net/ParksBlacklickWoods.aspx

Finding the trailhead: Take Interstate 270 to the East Main Street/Reynoldsburg exit. Drive east on Main Street and turn right onto Brice Road. Go down Brice Road and turn left at Livingston Avenue. Drive 1.4 miles and look for the park entrance on your right. Park at the Ash Grove Picnic Area, on the west side of the park entrance. GPS coordinates: N56 32.32' / W82 48.77'

The Hike

Blacklick Woods officially opened to the public in 1948, making it the oldest metro park in the system. Its combination of paved multiuse trails for joggers and dogs and mostly untouched forestland nestled within a nature preserve also make it one of the region's busiest metro parks. The park currently receives nearly one million visitors a year.

Blacklick features easy, flat terrain punctuated with

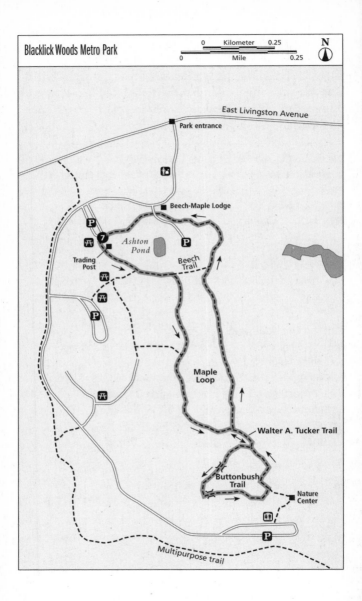

historic swamp forest and varied tree life. The first public park in the area, Blacklick Woods was successful despite the fact that it was inconveniently located away from the city and surrounding urban areas. Formerly an isolated park surrounded by farmland and visited by little more than a handful of bird-watchers and naturalists, today the park is surrounded by Reynoldsburg and an endless supply of housing developments and apartment complexes.

To get an in-depth look at what Blacklick Woods Metro Park has to offer, make a loop from Beech Trail to Maple Loop to Buttonbush Trail. During your hike you'll discover Blacklick Creek flowing south along the eastern perimeter of the park.

Start at the trailhead off the parking lot in the Ash Grove Picnic Area. Walk southeast toward the Old Trading Post building, the oldest structure built by the metro parks district. During operating hours, take a look inside to see some of the history of Blacklick and its original park plan. Afterwards, walk past the restrooms and playground and look for the Beech Trail sign.

Keep walking along Beech Trail until you reach the Maple Trail sign on your right at 0.1 mile. The gravel path is easy to follow and offers varied leaf litter and expansive views of the forest. Continue following the trail signs marked with leaf emblems that match symbols on the park's free maps. As you get closer to the nature preserve, you may find several vernal pools, especially after a heavy rain. These pools and the surrounding swamp area support a diversity of life, including salamanders, fairy shrimp, crustaceans, fingernail clams, burrowing crayfish, and of course plenty of insects.

At 0.6 mile turn right for the Walter A. Tucker Trail, which will link you directly to the Buttonbush Trail loop.

This area encompasses the fifty-four-acre Walter A. Tucker Scenic Nature Preserve, named for the founding director of the Columbus and Franklin County Metropolitan Park District. Tucker also helped to establish the state nature preserve system.

The preserve's relatively untouched forest helped put Blacklick on the map as a "watchable wildlife" location by the Ohio Division of Wildlife. Its seemingly remote and intimate setting leaves hikers to explore relatively undisturbed except for a few foxes or raccoons edging their way onto the trail.

Continue on the Walter A. Tucker Trail and pick up the Buttonbush Trail. Keep winding your way through the forest over the wooden boardwalks peppered with bursts of gravel paths. As the boardwalk zigzags through the park, you'll get an in-depth sampling of the swamp forest and its seasonal wildlife.

During migration periods, keep an eye out for woodpeckers, wrens, flycatchers, thrushes, and warblers nesting in the trees. This wetter region of Blacklick Woods Metro Park contains an interesting collection of white and pin oak, white ash, red maple, red elm, bur oak, shagbark and bitternut hickory, dogwood, spicebush, and buttonbush communities.

If you're wondering why the preserve considers the swamp forest its jewel, it's important to note that cornfields once surrounded these forests and the forests were typically harvested for their timber. In the mid to late 1800s, the federal government heavily promoted wetland drainage and reclamation for future settlement and development, which furthered the destruction of swamp forests nationwide.

Farmers were also prone to draining prairies and fields of their vernal pools in order to expand their agricultural opportunities. It was unique for the former owners of

Blacklick Woods, the Ashton family, to preserve the area rather than harvest and destroy it. As a result, Blacklick is one of the few areas in central Ohio that can still boast a substantial swamp-forest community and offer a depiction of the land as it was some 200 years ago.

After getting a sense of the history of the swampland, you can turn right at 1.0 mile to visit the nature center for more information about Blacklick Woods, area wildlife, and educational programs. To continue your hike, bear left. At 1.1 miles turn right to return to the Walter A. Tucker Trail and backtrack to again pick up the Maple Trail loop. At 1.2 miles turn right and start walking past the Blacklick Golf Course on your right.

Pick up Beech Trail again at 1.5 miles, and turn right to make your way past the Beech-Maple Lodge on your right. After you cross the road and resume the paved trail, return to the parking lot and trailhead.

Miles and Directions

0.0 Start at the trailhead past the Old Trading Post and playground.

0.1 Turn right for Maple Trail.

0.6 Turn right for Walter A. Tucker Trail.

0.8 Continue walking on gravel path and boardwalks.

1.0 Bear left at the fork. (Option: Turn right to visit the nature center.)

1.1 Turn right to return to the Walter A. Tucker Trail and back-track to Maple Trail.

1.2 Bear right and walk past Blacklick Golf Course.

1.5 Pick-up Beech Trail again, and turn right to make your way past the Beech-Maple Lodge on your right.

1.9 Arrive back at the trailhead.

8 Blendon Woods Metro Park

Hike through oak-hickory and beech-maple forests along stream-cut ravines in a park renowned for its birding activity.

Distance: 1.6-mile loop
Approximate hiking time: 1 hour
Difficulty: Easy
Trail surface: Gravel and dirt
Best season: March through November
Other trail users: None
Canine compatibility: Leashed dogs permitted on separate Goldenrod Pet Trail
Schedule: Open 6:30 a.m. to 10:00 p.m. April through September; 6:30 a.m. to 8:00 p.m. October through March
Maps: USGS Northeast Columbus
Trail contacts: Columbus Metro Parks, 4265 E. Dublin-Granville Road, Westerville, OH 43081; (614) 895-6221; http://metroparks.net/ParksBlendon Woods.aspx

Finding the trailhead: Take Interstate 270 to exit 30B for Route 161 toward New Albany, onto East Dublin-Granville Road. Drive 1.6 miles and exit at Little Turtle Way. Turn right and drive to Old Route 161. Turn right and continue 0.5 mile to the park entrance on your left. Park at the lot adjacent to the nature center. GPS coordinates: N4 16.89' / W82 52.40'

The Hike

Opened in 1951, 650-acre Blendon Woods Metro Park features stream-cut ravines nestled between beech-maple and oak-hickory forests. The park includes the 118-acre Walden Waterfowl Refuge with its 11-acre lake. This spot is popular with bird-watchers, who come here year-round. Observation shelters off Thoreau Lake also attract locals

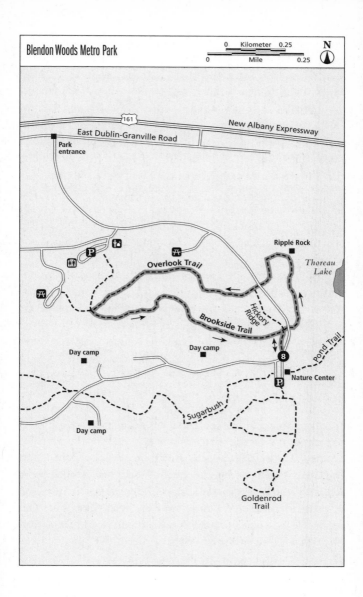

during migration periods for ducks, geese, herons, eastern kingbirds, as well as other birds.

Before your hike, visit the nature center tucked just off Pond Trail, which is adjacent to the parking lot. Ask the naturalist on duty about borrowing a set of binoculars for use inside the park and learn more about the bird migrations. You'll find plenty of wide observation windows with prime bird and wildlife viewing opportunities, including the rufous hummingbird and dickcissel. The center also can supply hikers with free maps, wildlife information, and information on upcoming programs in the park. On your way out, stop to observe the trees in front of the center, which are popular haunts for birds looking for a meal at the many feeders.

From the nature center, birding enthusiasts can traverse the 0.3-mile hike down to Thoreau Lake and visit the observation decks and shelters. But for a wider scope of Blendon Woods and a heartier hike, walk north from the parking lot to pick up Hickory Ridge Trail and make a loop through the beech-maple and oak-hickory forests. Starting at the trailhead off the parking lot, turn right for Ripple Rock Trail and cross a road before winding left into woods. This area contains a variety of northern red oak. Keep following along the gravel and dirt path, gently sloping through hills and along the creek.

At 0.1 mile cross another road; continue straight at the trail fork to access the Overlook Trail. You'll understand where this trail gets its name as you hike along the overlook of a stream-cut ravine and winding creek to your right. This particular leg of the hike offers the best views and feels completely removed from the urban bustle of the city.

Continue your hike and cross another road near Thoreau Lake. Keep an ear out for the songs of visiting chipping sparrows, rusty blackbirds, and mallards. At 0.6 mile look for the wooden and dirt steps leading down to a short bridge over a creek. From here begin sloping your way back up the hill and keep bearing left. You should see a picnic pavilion with a triangular roof and a playground area on your right. This heavily canopied area is an ideal spot for a rest or a picnic while watching for resident birds.

As you walk deeper into the forest, you might pick up on the contemplative and secluded atmosphere of Blendon Woods. The rolling forest features bursts of outcroppings of exposed bedrock, offering a sharp contrast to the deeply cut ravines. The park utilizes the area's moody quality by offering full-moon hikes and winter walks.

At 1.0 mile turn left to take the Brookside Trail. Hike across another small wooden bridge at 1.2 miles before continuing to make your way uphill. End your loop by turning right and returning to the parking lot.

Miles and Directions

0.0 Start at the trailhead and walk through the woods, crossing a road.

0.1 Cross a road and continue straight at the fork for the Overlook Trail.

0.5 Cross another road.

0.6 Walk down the wooden and dirt steps and over a bridge.

1.0 Turn left to pick up the Brookside Trail.

1.2 Cross a small wooden bridge and walk uphill.

1.6 Turn right to return to the trailhead.

⑨ Chestnut Ridge Metro Park: Ridge and Meadows Trails

Hike along a ridge trail more than 150 feet high offering dazzling views of the Columbus skyline from the observation deck, blackhand sandstone, and woodland beauty.

Distance: 1.9-mile loop

Approximate hiking time: 1 to 1.5 hours

Difficulty: Moderate due to frequent hills

Trail surface: Gravel and dirt

Best season: April through November and after a snowfall

Other trail users: Cross-country skiers

Canine compatibility: Dogs not permitted

Schedule: Open daily 6:30 a.m. to dark

Maps: USGS Canal Winchester

Trail contacts: Columbus Metro Parks, 8445 Winchester Road N.W., Carroll, OH 43112; (614) 891-0700; http://metroparks.net/TrailsChestnutRidge.aspx

Finding the trailhead: Take Interstate 270 to U.S. Highway 33 east, going toward Lancaster. Drive about 10 miles and turn right onto Winchester Road at the traffic light. The park entrance is 3 miles on your left. Park at the first lot on your right. GPS coordinates: N48 24.30' / W82 45.35'

The Hike

The sloping ridge along the 486-acre Chestnut Ridge Metro Park is 4,500 feet long and considered the first ridge among the foothills of the Appalachian Mountains. As the park's name implies, the looming sandstone ridge was once covered with a thick forest of chestnut trees that were a valuable food source for Native Americans and locals. Unfortunately,

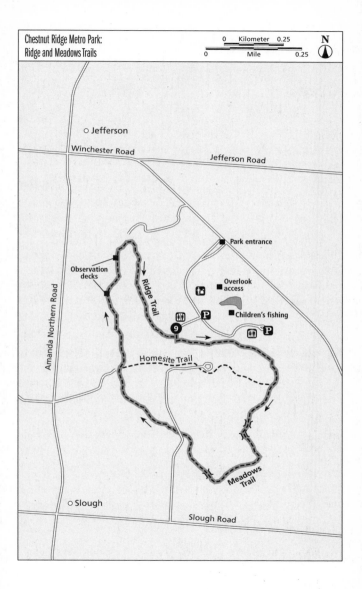

Chestnut Ridge Metro Park:
Ridge and Meadows Trails

0   Kilometer   0.25
0   Mile   0.25

N

○ Jefferson

Winchester Road   Jefferson Road

Amanda Northern Road

■ Park entrance

Observation
decks

Ridge Trail

Overlook
access

■ Children's fishing

P

9

Homesite Trail

Meadows
Trail

○ Slough

Slough Road

a deadly fungus from an imported tree or lumber infected and ultimately destroyed the area's chestnut trees.

Today hikers can traverse fields, woods, observation decks with city skyline views, and rolling hills among a diversity of plant and tree life. The upper and lower slopes each grow a unique community of trees to peruse along your hike. Look for shagbark hickory and northern red oaks along the upper slopes and sugar maples and American beech on the lower slopes.

To see the scope of the park's diversity, hike the Ridge Trail to Meadows Trail loop. Although the excursion is less than 2 miles, the continuously sloping hills make for a moderately challenging hike. Adventurous locals use the ridge and hiking trails to ready themselves before tackling the Appalachian Trail.

Find the trailhead just off the first parking lot from the park's main entrance, and bear left to begin the Ridge Trail. You'll see a sharp left for access to a parking lot, restrooms, and playgrounds. Keep straight, taking a moment to look around at the trees lining the trail. You should be able to spot a few black locust trees as the trail slopes uphill and curves right.

If you've already hiked several of the trails in the Columbus metro park system, you'll notice the sharp contrast in increased elevation while hiking through Chestnut Ridge. Compared to the easy, flat terrain in Blacklick Woods' swamp forest, this hike will feel positively hilly, if not altogether mountainous. During winter months, hikers will find themselves sharing the trails with cross-country skiers making the most of the sloping hills after a fresh snowfall.

While fall is prime hiking season to see bursts of vivid

color along the forest canopy, organized winter hikes are also popular and draw scores of hikers to many of the metro parks in the region. Although the snow can be troublesome on some of the steep hills in Chestnut Ridge, the city views of Columbus are well worth the effort. But winter also means missing out on much of the bird–viewing opportunities. In warmer months, listen for the park's some seventy species of birds, ranging from doves to warblers to owls, migrating through the open meadows and forest. Butterflies can also be found resting among the wildflowers and meadows.

At 0.4 mile turn left to continue along Meadows Trail. A right turn here will take you across the park via the Homesite Trail. The Homesite section of the park still houses the remains of Far View Farms, with the original fruit trees planted by the owners.

Keep walking along Meadows Trail, making your way out of the woods and through tall fields. Begin ascending the hill; bear right and cross a wooden bridge. At 1.2 miles you'll pass the other end of the Homesite Trail on your right. Continue straight until you reach the overlook decks and a wooden boardwalk at 1.6 miles. These are the jewels of the hike, with valley and city views of Columbus below.

It's unusual to have such vivid city views from any of the trails in the metro park system. Most of the system's trail terrain is heavily wooded and designed to give visitors a feeling of seclusion and a refuge from city life. Views of the Columbus skyline are an especially surprising find within Chestnut Ridge Metro Park, as the hike leading up to the overlook winds through open meadows and heavy forest. It remains one of the focal points of the park and offers a reminder of the balance between encroaching urbanization and the preservation of nature.

After enjoying the views from the ridge, traverse through the forest and walk along a wooden boardwalk until you resume the gravel path and continue downhill. Turn left at the fork to return to the parking lot. To avoid the additional hills, many hikers choose to start from this point, climb uphill to the observation deck, and then backtrack to the parking lot instead of making a full loop.

On your way out of the park, take a moment to stop at the ranger station and wetland overlook access area. Like most other Columbus metro parks, Chestnut Ridge works to preserve Ohio's wetlands. As you leave the parking lot after your hike, the wetland overlook entrance will be on your right, shortly before the park's main entrance. Watch for wood ducks, green herons, and mallards in the wetlands and on the two-acre pond.

Miles and Directions

- **0.0** Start at trailhead off the parking lot and bear left onto the Ridge Trail.
- **0.4** Turn left onto the Meadows Trail. (Option: Cut across the park via the Homesite Trail.)
- **1.2** Pass the other end of the Homesite Trail on your right. Continue straight.
- **1.6** Look for observation decks and boardwalk with views of Columbus.
- **1.9** Turn left at the fork to end the loop and arrive back at the parking lot.

10 Slate Run Metro Park: Kokomo Wetland Trail

Take a walk through some of Ohio's protected wetlands, explore a glacial outwash bank, and see migrating birds and more along the wetland boardwalk.

Distance: 1.4-mile loop
Approximate hiking time: 1 hour
Difficulty: Easy
Trail surface: Grass, gravel, dirt, wetlands, and boardwalk
Best season: April through October
Other trail users: None
Canine compatibility: Leashed dogs permitted only on Covered

Bridge and Shagbark pet trails
Schedule: Open daily 6:30 a.m. to dark
Maps: USGS Canal Winchester
Trail contacts: Metro parks, 1375 State Route 674 N. Canal, Winchester, OH 43110; (614) 508-8000; http://metroparks .net/MapSlateRun.aspx

Finding the trailhead: From Interstate 270, take U.S. Highway 33 east toward Lancaster to the Canal Winchester/Route 674 exit. Turn right onto Gender Road/SR 674 and go about 2 miles until it dead-ends into Lithopolis Road. Turn left and go about 0.5 mile to SR 674. Turn right and go about four miles to the entrance on the right. Continue past main park entrance 0.5 mile to Marcy Road and turn right. Go three miles to Winchester Road and turn right. Wetlands entrance is about 2 miles on the right. GPS coordinates: N45 52.92' / W82 51.93'

The Hike

Early settlers mistook the dark soil in the area now known as Slate Run Metro Park for ancient slate. Instead of slate, the park is actually home to a soft rock made from clay

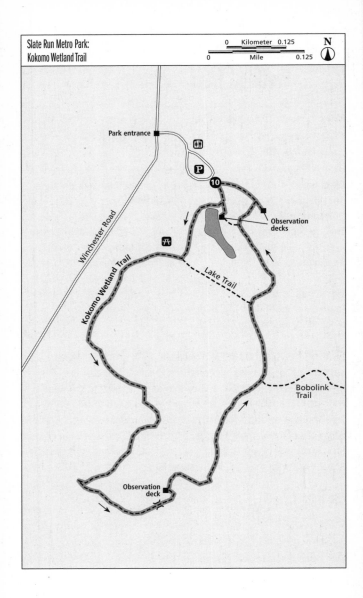

Slate Run Metro Park:
Kokomo Wetland Trail

Park entrance

Winchester Road

Kokomo Wetland Trail

10

Observation decks

Lake Trail

Bobolink Trail

Observation deck

0   Kilometer 0.125
0   Mile   0.125

N

deposited by water centuries ago. As was commonplace at the time, settlers drained most of Ohio's early wetlands for farming and timber resources. In addition to the draining, ongoing road and home construction also served to alter the state's water conditions.

Following an extensive study of soil and groundwater conditions, park naturalists now believe that the land in Slate Run was originally a wetland meadow. In 1995 and 1996 a portion of the park's grasslands were restored featuring Kentucky bluegrass, purple bergamot, butterfly milkweed, short fescue, and ashy sunflower.

In 1999 the Slate Run Wetlands Mitigation bank was completed, and the wetlands preserve opened to the public in 2000. The wetlands habitat features sedge meadow, scrub shrub, native prairie grasses, and remnant wooded fencerows. This was only the third such bank completed by the Ohio Wetlands Foundation in Central Ohio. The organization continues to restore and preserve the state's wetlands, and its work can be found in other Ohio parks, including Hebron, Big Island, Sandy Ridge, and Three Eagles.

The preservation efforts have paid off. Slate Run now attracts more than seventy species of birds, including indigo buntings, meadowlarks, wood ducks, northern harriers, redheaded woodpeckers, savannah sparrows, red-winged blackbirds, belted kingfishers, and numerous other birds and wildlife. Even when the wetlands' edges are splintered with ice after a winter snowfall, an occasional beaver can be seen swimming alongside the wooden boardwalks and fallen trees. In warmer months, Slate Run attracts visitors to its impressive butterfly community.

Get an up-close and personal view of the 156-acre wetland and its inhabitants with an easy hike around the

Kokomo Wetland Trail. Park at the Slate Run Wetlands Wildlife Refuge entrance and walk past the covered picnic pavilion to locate the trailhead sign. Turn right at the trailhead and loop through the grass-and-dirt path lined with tall grass. The wetland area was formed from a glacial outwash bank where sediment was deposited as the glacier melted. The trail can be especially muddy after rain and snow, so wear adequate boots and expect a more moderate hike in damp conditions.

As the trail snakes through the park, you'll notice a series of splintering forks to spur trails through the grass. Keep bearing right until you reach a fork at 0.6 mile. Turn left and make your way to the wooden boardwalks crossing over the water. As you hike through the wetlands, listen for nesting pip-billed grebes, green-winged teal, or migrating birds passing through. It's estimated that nearly half of Ohio's threatened and endangered species are dependent on wetland habitats. The state cooperates with countrywide conservation organizations to help protect the complex bird migration across North America.

After exploring the boardwalk and wetlands, continue hiking to a fork at 1.1 miles; turn left. You can also turn right to pick up the Bobolink Trail for access to Sugar Maple and Five Oaks Trails. This nearly 6.0-mile loop hike winds through the rest of Slate Run Metro Park and features hardwood forests and wildlife. This end of the park boasts forests of beech, oak, hickory, and sugar maple where hikers might spot white-tailed deer and owls.

Continue along Kokomo Wetland Trail. At 1.3 miles turn right and walk until you reach the paved path. From this point you can choose to end your hike or make your way over to the observation deck on your right for an overview of the wetlands and the forested region of the park. See if you can spot the hundred-year-old Osage orange tree near the Bobolink Trail spur.

For more information about wetlands and conservation, Slate Run offers educational programs and events open to the public. You can also see other Columbus metro park wetlands at Pickerington Ponds, Battelle Darby Creek, Highbanks, Prairie Oaks, Chestnut Ridge, Glacier Ridge, and Three Creeks. Overall, the park system works to preserve more than 1,000 acres of wetlands.

In addition to the park's 13 miles of trails, Slate Run also boasts a restored bridge from the 1800s and the Slate Run Living Historical Farm. The farm still uses wind energy and draft horses to help tell the story of life on a working 1880s farm. Food is prepared right on top of the wood-burning stove, kerosene lamps are used instead of electricity, and old-fashioned sewing machines can be found inside. Visitors can learn more about life on the 1880s farm and even help with chores.

Miles and Directions

0.0 Start at trailhead off the Slate Run Wetlands Wildlife Refuge parking lot.

0.6 Bear left at the fork.

0.8 Walk over the boardwalk and observation outlooks.

1.1 Pass the Bobolink trailhead on your right.

1.3 Turn right and continue to the paved path and observation deck area.

1.4 Arrive back at the trailhead and return to the parking lot.

11 North Bank Park

Take a walk along the Scioto River in downtown Columbus for skyline views, outdoor pavilions, an interactive museum, and a touch of history.

Distance: 1.6-mile loop
Approximate hiking time: 1.5 hours; longer with museum stop
Difficulty: Easy
Trail surface: Paved
Best season: March through November
Other trail users: Bicyclists and in-line skaters
Canine compatibility: Leashed dogs permitted
Schedule: Open daily 8:00 a.m. to 11:00 p.m.
Maps: USGS Southwest Columbus
Trail contacts: Columbus Department of Recreation and Parks, 1111 East Broad Street, Columbus, OH 43205; (614) 645-3300; http://recparks .columbus.gov

Finding the trailhead: Take U.S. Highway 33 in downtown Columbus. Park at West Long Street and Neil Avenue at the parking meters in front of the North Bank Park Pavilion. GPS coordinates: N57 55.00' / W83 00.55'

The Hike

North Bank Park lies just north of downtown Columbus and in front of the city's Arena and Pen West Districts. A member of the Scioto Mile network of downtown parks, North Bank is a part of Mayor Michael B. Coleman's plan to revitalize Columbus's downtown to attract visitors and locals alike. Paved trails from the north connect the park to the Olentangy and Scioto Greenway Trails. To the south, visitors can walk to Battelle Riverfront Park, Bicentennial Parks, and Avenue of Flags.

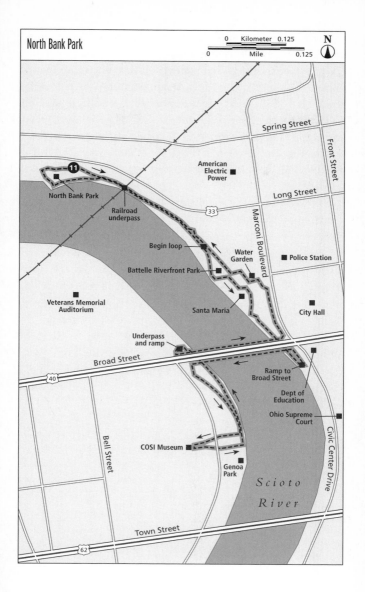

North Bank Park

| 0 | Kilometer | 0.125 |
| 0 | Mile | 0.125 |

N

Spring Street

Front Street

American Electric Power

Long Street

33

North Bank Park

Railroad underpass

Begin loop

Water Garden

Marconi Boulevard

Police Station

Battelle Riverfront Park

Veterans Memorial Auditorium

Santa Maria

City Hall

Underpass and ramp

Broad Street

40

Ramp to Broad Street

Dept of Education

Bell Street

Ohio Supreme Court

Civic Center Drive

COSI Museum

Genoa Park

Scioto River

Town Street

62

The city of Columbus bolstered North Bank's opening in 2005 by showcasing a variety of events, including "Water Fire on the Mile," named for the mile of the Scioto River. The city organized a floating bonfire display along the river and featured street performers, dancers, and music to entertain the crowd. North Bank Park is also renowned for its innovative design. In 2007 local architect firms Acock Associates Architects and HKI Associates won the James B. Recchie Design Award for their work on the park and pavilion.

Today the park's events are generally clustered around the pavilion along West Long Street and the outdoor amphitheater in front of the COSI Museum. The museum area features water fountains, a panoramic view of downtown, lawns, paved trails, and room to lounge. Across the water from COSI lies the impressive state supreme court building. Just a few decades ago, evening laser shows danced across its walls to entertain crowds from where COSI sits today.

Start your hike at the North Bank Park Pavilion on West Long Street and Neil Avenue, where you'll find parking meters, public restrooms, benches, a fountain, and a lawn. Walk around the pavilion to your right and onto the paved path. Walk parallel to the water.

During the hike, stop to read some of the signs scattered throughout the park's central region with information about Columbus's history. The park itself embodies a touch of the city's more sordid history. Take a look at the limestone along the park's walls. Some of it was salvaged from the former Ohio Penitentiary that once stood just north of the park.

As you being your hike, walk under a rail overpass and slope uphill. This area enters into Battelle Riverfront Park, which is also a part of the Columbus Department of Recreation and Parks. This urban park houses a small amphitheater, boat launch access, gardens and floral displays, and access to the Greenway Trail. In addition to a picnic pavilion, a large colonial-style ship can usually be found resting along the river's banks at about 0.3 mile. The ship is part of *Santa Maria* tours and offers passenger rides along the Scioto River. You can make your way upstairs to the street or keep going straight to continue this hike.

Cross under the stone bridge. At the end of the pathway, loop back and walk upstairs to Broad Street (0.4 mile). From here you can see the Ohio supreme court building just across the street on your right. Turn left and cross the river on the Broad Street Bridge. While there is a sidewalk dedicated to pedestrian use, watch for bicycles and cars on the road next to you.

At 0.6 mile turn left and walk downstairs to the paved trail along the water. Make your way to the flags and pavilion area just below the COSI science museum. This is an ideal spot to take in views of the skyline or sit along the water's edge and enjoy a picnic. You can also explore the outdoor amphitheater and steps leading up to the COSI Museum.

COSI's intriguing building was once home to Columbus's Central High School, and the museum incorporates part of the original infrastructure. The original staircase remains, and the former high school entrance is located at the museum's eastern entrance. The high school remained in operation from the 1920s until it closed in 1982. Today the school and its alumni are featured in a showcased museum exhibit. If you're hiking with kids, spend a few hours exploring the expansive kid-friendly science museum, interactive exhibits, and educational programs.

After your visit to COSI, make your way back down the steps you came up. When you reach 0.9 mile at the bottom of the steps, you can turn right to walk to the end of the paved trail near the next underpass or turn left to continue this hike. Keep walking along the water, taking in the views of the skyline. Continue underneath the bridge and make a sharp left up the stairs to Broad Street. From here you're walking across the other side of the bridge you crossed earlier.

At the end of the bridge (1.2 miles), turn left and walk through the upper plaza area of Battelle Riverfront Park. You'll find a water garden with fountains, a firefighters memorial with an eternal flame, and plaques with information about sponsors who helped build the area. Small statues of lions, giraffes, and other animals near the fountain help keep kids entertained.

Continue along the upper plaza and make your way back to the North Bank Park Pavilion and brick walkway. You will approach the pavilion from behind and discover plenty of benches and opportunity for views of the water and skyline. Walk back to the front of the pavilion to end your hike.

Miles and Directions

0.0 Start at the North Bank Park Pavilion. Walk around the pavilion to your right and onto the paved path.

0.2 Enter the Battelle Riverfront Park area.

0.3 Reach the dock along the waterfront.

0.4 Walk up steps to Broad Street.

0.5 Turn left at Broad Street and cross a bridge over the river.

0.6 Reach the end of the street; turn left and walk downstairs.

- **0.7** Reach the amphitheater and walk up the steps to COSI Museum.
- **0.9** Return to the bottom of the steps from COSI, and turn left.
- **1.0** Turn left and go up the steps to return to Broad Street.
- **1.2** Turn left and walk along the upper plaza of Battelle Riverfront Park.
- **1.3** Stop to view the water garden.
- **1.6** Arrive back at the North Bank Park Pavilion.

12 A. W. Marion State Park: Hargus Lake Trail

Hike among the rolling hills around Hargus Lake for forested trails that are home to red foxes, ring-necked pheasants, Canada geese, turtles, and white-tailed deer.

Distance: 3.8-mile loop
Approximate hiking time: 2 hours
Difficulty: Moderate due to hills
Trail surface: Flat dirt and some mud
Best season: April through October
Other trail users: Seasonal hunters
Canine compatibility: Leashed dogs permitted
Schedule: Open daily until 11:00 p.m.
Maps: USGS Ashville
Trail contacts: A. W. Marion State Park, c/o Deer Creek State Park, 20635 Waterloo Road, Mount Sterling 43143; (740) 869-3124; www.dnr.state.oh.us/parks/parks/awmarion/tabid/712/Default.aspx

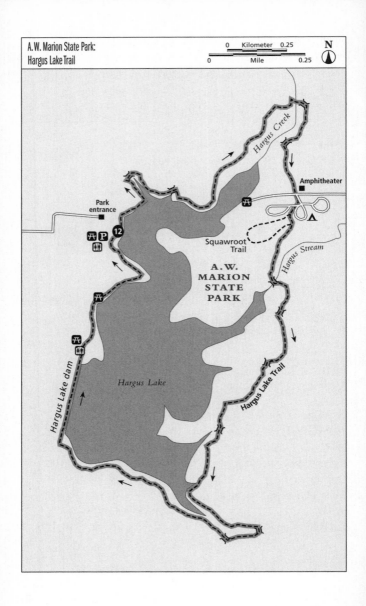

A.W. Marion State Park:
Hargus Lake Trail

0   Kilometer   0.25

0   Mile   0.25

N

Hargus Creek

Amphitheater

Park
entrance

12

Squawroot
Trail

A.W.
MARION
STATE
PARK

Hargus Stream

Hargus Lake dam

Hargus Lake

Hargus Lake Trail

Finding the trailhead: From Route 23 in Chillicothe, turn east onto U.S. Highway 22. Drive 2.3 miles and turn left onto Bolender-Pontius Road, marked with a brown state park sign. Go 1.5 miles and turn right onto Warner-Huffer Road. Drive 0.4 mile to a T intersection and take a right on Warner-Huffer Road. Continue 0.2 mile to the park entrance, and turn left into the parking lot. GPS coordinates: N37 59.16' / W82 53.03'

The Hike

Ancient glacial activity helped create the present-day A. W. Marion State Park and the surrounding Till Plains ecoregion. Like many of the wetland areas and native forests of Ohio, the land was drained and converted to farmland by white settlers. The 145-acre Hargus Lake remains—a focal point for recreation and relaxation. The park features wooded terrain, rolling hills, winding creeks, an elevated rim, and a few small islands.

The nearby city of Circleville has a lengthy history of Shawnee influence. The city was named for the circular Adena earthworks discovered in the region. Early inhabitants originally came to the area for the fertile soil of the Pickaway Plains, thought to be the richest land in Ohio. White settlers eventually cleared and cultivated the land for agricultural use. A Revolutionary War cemetery still remains in the area and is cared for by the local historical society.

Hargus Lake was eyed for its potential recreational use, and construction for a dam commenced in 1948. In 1950 the area officially became part of the newly founded Division of Parks and Recreation, and in 1962 the park was named for the first director of the Ohio Department of Natural Resources, A. W. Marion. Today the park is a popular spot for both locals and visitors looking for boat rentals, fishing, bird watching, picnicking, and hiking.

The park is also a popular gathering spot for white-tailed deer, red foxes, ring-necked pheasants, and fox squirrels. You can also see evidence of Canada geese flocking on the west side of the lake. Regardless of where you are on the trail, be careful where you step. During peak season it's nearly impossible not to step directly into the geese's calling card.

Although an easy hike, Hargus Lake does have numerous hills of various inclines. A recent rainstorm will make the trail difficult to manage, as the dirt terrain quickly turns to slick mud. Creek crossings with cinder blocks and stepping-stones are frequent along this hike. You'll also find that the hike beautifully blends woodlands, plains, prairies, and recreational opportunities.

Start hiking from the well-marked trailhead sign to the left of the boat rental house and docks, just off the parking lot and restrooms. Walk clockwise through the woods and follow the blue blazes marked directly on the trees. You'll cross from a grassy path onto dirt and quickly find yourself enveloped in a thick forest canopy.

At 0.2 mile walk down the wooden steps to a small bridge. You will cross several bridges on this hike, with or without cinder blocks or dry stepping-stones. However, the creek is narrow and can be crossed without too much difficulty. For areas where the creek widens, short wooden bridges are available. An extra pair of dry socks and change of shoes stashed in your car is a good idea.

When you were at the trailhead sign off the parking lot, you might have noticed that the line of forest cover completely etches around the perimeter of the lake. At first glance, you might think you're going to parallel the lake and enjoy water views for the entire hike. But during the hike you'll be surprised to find increasing elevation and infrequent views of the lake against the maple, hickory, oak, and beech trees. Before this region was settled, scrub oak barrens and shrubs were commonplace but were eventually cleared to raise crops.

At 1.2 miles climb uphill until you reach the small amphitheater on your left, used for park and educational programs. The trail can be a little tricky to follow from this point. Walk through the campground, past the small building on your left, and continue through the campsite markers. Walk through the campground and note the Squawroot Trail marker at 1.3 miles. Keep walking and access the Hargus Lake Trail, marked with blue blazes and a trailhead sign. Locating the marker for Campsite 24 should also bring the sign into view.

As you reach the east side of the lake, note the small but prominent ridge overlooking the lake. Once called Devil's Backbone, this is a popular spot for turtle watching and catching a glimpse of the lake and forest below. Cross a short wooden bridge at 1.5 miles, and continue until you walk down a set of wooden and dirt stairs at 2.0 miles.

Wind right and walk uphill until you see views of the forest and lake below. At 2.6 miles you'll come across a barn and private residence. Bear right and keep paralleling the lake. Keep walking through a grassy meadow region alongside the lake. You'll probably see several fishing access trails leading to the lake, made by anglers looking for a fresh catch. With a valid Ohio fishing license, you can fish for black crappie, bluegill, chain pickerel, channel catfish, carp, and largemouth bass.

Make your way back to the recreational area and parking lot, passing the Hargus Lake dam at 3.2 miles. Keep walking through the series of picnic pavilions, restrooms, and the boat rental until you're back to the trailhead.

Miles and Directions

0.0 Start the Hargus Lake Trail sign near the parking lot and walk clockwise.

0.2 Cross two wooden bridges.

1.2 Walk uphill and look for the amphitheater on your left.

1.3 Pass the inner Squawroot Trail.

1.5 Cross a bridge over Hargus Stream.

2.0 Walk downhill and over wooden steps.

2.6 Pass a barn and private residence, bear right.

3.2 Pass the Hargus Lake dam.

3.3 Walk past a series of picnic pavilions and restrooms.

3.8 Arrive back at the trailhead.

13 Clear Creek Metro Park

Drive past "Leaning Leena" and hike along Clear Creek before ascending through a forest and accessing a secluded rim trail.

Distance: 3.6-mile loop
Approximate hiking time: 2.5 hours
Difficulty: Moderate due to hills
Trail surface: Dirt
Best season: April through October
Other trail users: None
Canine compatibility: Leashed

dogs permitted on separate Barneby Pet Trail
Schedule: Open daily from 6:30 a.m. until dark
Maps: USGS Rockbridge
Trail contacts: Columbus Metro Parks, 185 Clear Creek Road, Rockbridge, OH 43149; (614) 508-8000; www.metroparks.net

Finding the trailhead: From U.S. Highway 33 between Lancaster and Logan, turn west onto County Road 116 (Clear Creek Road), marked with a small brown sign. Drive about 2.5 miles to the Creekside Meadows Picnic Area on your left. The trailhead is on the east side of the parking lot. GPS coordinates: N35 19.97' / W82 34.68'

The Hike

Clear Creek Metro Park, one of the most pristine parks in the Columbus metro park system, is often overlooked. Located about 30 miles southeast of the Interstate 270 outer belt in the Hocking Hills region, the park is a jaunt for a day hike from Columbus. But for those looking for a hiking alternative from the city's urban setting, Clear Creek provides a secluded atmosphere tucked away in the wilderness.

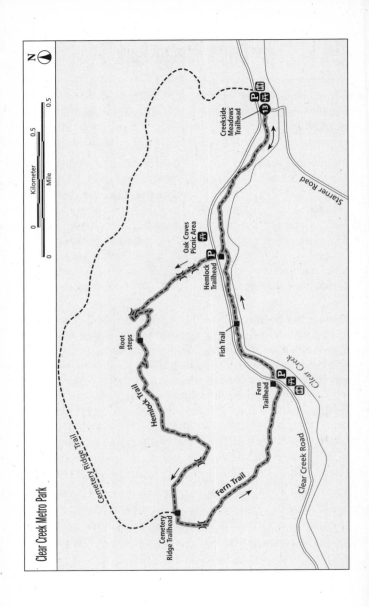

Clear Creek Metro Park

N

Cemetery Ridge Trail

Root steps

Hemlock Trail

Oak Coves Picnic Area

Hemlock Trailhead

Fish Trail

Cemetery Ridge Trailhead

Fern Trail

Fern Trailhead

Clear Creek

Clear Creek Road

Starner Road

Creekside Meadows Trailhead

13

Kilometer
0   0.5

0   0.5
Mile

For visitors who have never ventured beyond Columbus's urban parks, the Hocking Hills area will look foreign. It's believed that the Wisconsinan glacier made its way into Clear Creek Valley centuries ago. Glacial flooding helped cut through the blackhand sandstone, which is common in this region, to form the valley. The area's rugged topography brings tourists and hikers looking to explore its breathtaking cliffs and rugged rocks overlooking the creek.

You can see one of the more popular rock formations without ever leaving your car. The Leaning Leena won't be difficult to find. As you're driving down Clear Creek Road to the parking lot, you might feel a need to duck as you cruise past this towering rock.

During the late 1960s plans to dam the valley and turn it into a reservoir surfaced. Fortunately the proposal was quashed and the Beck and Benua families who owned land in the valley began donating it to Franklin County Metro Parks. The two families had been renowned for acquiring and preserving the valley for decades. Oscar Barneby also owned valley land, which later became a natural resources lab for Ohio State University.

Current plans for Clear Creek Metro Park are to keep it in its semiprimitive state, with areas closed to the public to preserve rare and endangered species. However, there are plans to develop more permanent trails, picnic pavilions, and spots for nature program presentations.

To get a sampling of what the park has to offer, start your hike at the Creekside Meadows parking lot. To find the trailhead, walk east until you see the sign for Creekside Meadows Trail. This portion of the hike is flat, with a dirt-and-gravel path lined with tall grasses that follows along Clear Creek. You'll find fishing access points in this area for anglers looking for brown trout, rock bass, and smallmouth bass.

Cross the road at 0.5 mile and pick up Hemlock Trail, named for the hemlocks in the area. You will also see a variety of ferns, including ebony spleenwort, polyploidy, Christmas, wood, and maidenhair. Overall, some 1,200 species of plants grow in the Clear Creek region, including little gray horsetail, pink lady's slipper, mountain laurel, skunk cabbage, witch hazel, and American chestnut and persimmon trees. The trails and deep woods quickly envelop hikers in relative seclusion.

The ascent up the 300-foot ridge might come as a surprise after the flat hike along Creekside Meadows Trail. But hikers are rewarded as Hemlock Trail showcases rugged, steep ravines; cliff faces; and rock outcroppings. Although the distance of this hike is relatively short, it remains a pleasant challenge.

During your climb to the ridge, you should still catch glimpses of the creek snaking through the lower portion of the trail, with infrequent small wooden bridges around 0.7 and 0.9 mile. Beaver activity is common here, and chipmunks have an affinity for hiding under the leaf litter and exposed roots of the trees. Watch your step.

Continue the ascent and take note of the nearly 150 species of birds, some which are rare. That number makes up nearly half the 300 bird species that call Ohio home each year. Listen for eastern bluebirds, veeries, warblers, woodcocks, herons, wood thrushes, and a few black vultures in the treetops.

As you reach the top of the ridge, you will be treated to views of the valley floor and surrounding area. Elusive bobcats are known to live along the rock ledges, but sightings are rare. Continue walking and make the gradual descent to the fork at 1.9 miles for Cemetery Ridge and Fern Trails. This area is a popular spot for mountain laurel and reindeer moss. Turn left to continue along Fern Trail, or turn right for a more strenuous hike.

Keep descending down the trail and walk over a wooden bridge at 2.0 miles before crossing the road to the Fern Picnic Area. At the parking lot, bear left and walk along the narrow, grassy trail until you reach the road. It may not seem obvious where the trail continues. Just turn right at the trail marker at 2.8 miles and follow along the road, being careful to watch for cars. Although off the grass and dirt trails, hikers will have lovely views of the creek to the right. Once you pass the sign for fishing access, locate the FERN TRAIL sign leading back into the woods.

Continue to walk along the creek and make your way back to the Creekside Meadows Picnic Area. Walk past the trailhead sign and back to the parking lot.

Miles and Directions

0.0 Start at Creekside Meadows parking lot.

0.5 Cross the road and pick up Hemlock Trail.

0.7 Cross a wooden bridge.

0.9 Cross a wooden bridge.

1.1 Walk along rootlike steps.

1.9 Pick up Fern Trail.

2.0 Cross a wooden bridge.

2.6 Cross a road to pick up Fern Trail.

2.8 Turn right at the trail marker and walk along road and creek.

2.9 At fishing access point, look for the FERN TRAIL sign leading back into the woods.

3.6 Arrive back at the trailhead and parking lot.

14 Conkle's Hollow State Nature Preserve: Rim and Gorge Trails

Hike along the rim of the hollow for sandstone overlooks, rock outcroppings, and tumbling waterfalls on one of the best scenic trails in Ohio. Afterwards, hike through the belly of the gorge for a look at the caves, grotto, and springtime wildflowers below.

Distance: Rim Trail, 2.0-mile loop; Gorge Trail, 1.2-mile loop

Approximate hiking time: 2.5 hours for Rim Trail, 1 hour for Gorge Trail to 3 hours for combined trails

Difficulty: Rim Trail, moderate due to a steep ascent and rocky trail; Gorge Trail, paved and easy

Trail surface: Rim Trail, dirt and rock; Gorge Trail, paved

Best season: April through November

Other trail users: None

Canine compatibility: Dogs not permitted

Schedule: Open dawn to dusk year-round

Maps: USGS South Bloomingville

Trail contacts: Conkle's Hollow State Nature Preserve, 24858 Big Pine Road, Rockbridge, OH 43149; (740) 380-8919; www.dnr.state.oh.us/Home/ preserves_main/conkles_hollow/ tabid/884/Default.aspx

Finding the trailhead: From U.S. Highway 33 in Logan, turn south on Route 664 and drive 11.8 miles to the Hocking Hills State Visitor Center. From here drive another 1.6 miles to a T intersection connecting to Route 274. Turn right onto Route 274 and travel 1.0 mile. Turn right onto Big Pine Road and drive 0.2 mile to the parking lot on your left. GPS coordinates: N27 12.75' / W82 34.40'

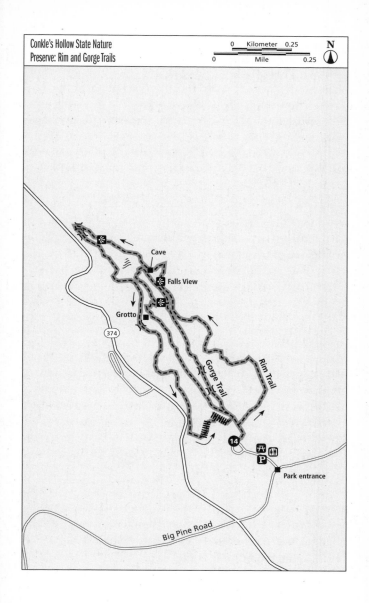

Conkle's Hollow State Nature
Preserve: Rim and Gorge Trails

0   Kilometer   0.25
0   Mile   0.25

N

Cave

Falls View

Grotto

374

Gorge Trail

Rim Trail

14

P

Park entrance

Big Pine Road

The Hike

Conkle's Hollow is one of the more unusual and scenic hiking spots in the entire Hocking Hills region. The park features towering cliffs of blackhand sandstone rising some 200 feet from the valley floor, a narrow rim trail, waterfalls, caves, and a grotto.

The hollow was named for one of the earliest visitors to the gorge, W. J. Conkle. He carved his name and the date 1797 into the western wall. The hollow itself is composed of ancient layers of blackhand sandstone that were eroded by water over the centuries to create the deep ravine. The area for the park was purchased by the state of Ohio in 1925 in an ongoing effort to preserve its scenic beauty. In 1977 the site became an official state nature preserve.

The valley floor features ferns and nearly fifty species of wildflowers. The upper region is home to birch and hemlocks. The forest cover can reach intense densities that make it difficult for sunlight to pass to the bottom of the gorge. The result down below is a cool and damp environment with a peppering of wildflowers and bright leaf litter along the cavernous rock walls.

Hikers should be advised that while the upper trail isn't too difficult to hike, the rocky rim can be narrow and there are no safety fences or guardrails along this section. Even seasoned hikers should exercise extreme caution while maneuvering along the rim's edges. The rim itself is only 100 to 300 feet wide in some areas and offers spectacular views of the gorge's depth and tumbling waterfalls. Children and anyone nervous about heights should probably skip the rim hike. Instead stick to the easy, paved Gorge Trail, which cuts through the bottom of the gorge.

Start your hike at the trailhead sign at the north end of the parking lot, just off the wheelchair-accessible parking area. The start of this hike carries you over a bridge and bends left into the forest. The trail quickly changes from Hocking Hills State Park to Conkle's Hollow Nature Preserve. Hikers choosing to just walk through the belly of the gorge should walk straight at the LOWER GORGE TRAIL sign and skip down to that section of the hike description. Otherwise turn right and walk up the wooden steps and steep incline toward the rim.

As the stairs end, continue walking along the narrow, root-filled trail. It will quickly turn rocky and narrow as you continue uphill. The series of makeshift rocky steps and stairs will carry you through the east side of the rim. Opportunities for views across the valley abound, with large rock overhangs affording a closer look at the gorge and surrounding preserve.

During the hike, keep an eye out for an ancient marking on the eastern wall. Local legend tells of Native Americans hiding money in a small opening on the gorge's west wall after stealing it from white settlers rafting down the Ohio River. To reach the opening in the recess cave and squirrel away the money, the Native Americans chopped down a tall hemlock tree to use as a ladder. The story goes that they chiseled an arrow on the eastern wall to point to the hidden money on the gorge's western wall and pushed the hemlock ladder into the gorge so it couldn't be used again. A storm knocked down a second tree intended for the money's retrieval before the Native Americans could return for their stash. The money was never found, but early settlers and older locals claim to have seen the carved arrow. Whether truth or folklore, the carving is no longer visible; the cash might still remain inside the gorge today.

Continue hiking, stopping to take in the astonishing views of a cascading waterfall that will reveal itself against the rock wall at 1.0 mile. While there are several smaller waterfalls along the hike, this is the focal point of the Rim Trail. After the waterfall, cross a small bridge and make a sharp left at 1.1 miles. You should see a rope blocking off the trail directly in front of the bridge. The land beyond the rope is not part of the rim hike. Instead, make the sharp left to begin your walk along the western wall of the gorge.

Continue hiking, taking a moment to look back at the views of the waterfall from the west side. At 1.9 miles you'll come to a view of the road and steps leading down to a dirt trail. After reaching the bottom of the gorge, turn left to walk the 0.5-mile lower Gorge Trail to see the sights from below.

This easy, paved trail snakes through the valley floor of the gorge. Visitors can see how the soft sandstone eroded faster than the surrounding rock, leaving behind quirky recesses and caves. At 0.4 mile, look for a small grotto in the rock wall. A nearby sign suggests that the inside of the grotto resembles a large horse head. Consequently, it's often called Horse Head Grotto. A combination of dancing moonlit shadows and the shrill cry of screech owls makes it an eerie spot at twilight.

When the paved path ends, you can either loop back to the original trailhead and parking lot or continue along the dirt nature trail and under the recess of rocks and ledges. It's well worth the effort, as the end of the trail reveals waterfalls cascading to the stream along the gorge floor. Over the noise of the water, listen for nesting songbirds. Once you've finished exploring the gorge, loop back and return to the parking lot to end your hike.

Miles and Directions

Rim Trail

0.0 Start at the trailhead near the wheelchair-accessible parking lot and walk up the stairs to the east rim trail.

1.0 View a tumbling waterfall.

1.1 Cross a bridge and turn sharply left to access the east rim trail.

1.4 Cross another bridge.

1.9 Walk down the stairs.

2.0 Reach the end of the rim hike. Arrive back at the trailhead, or continue on the Gorge Trail.

Gorge Trail

0.0 Start at the trailhead near the wheelchair-accessible parking lot, and go straight at the sign for the Gorge Trail.

0.2 Cross a bridge.

0.4 Stop by a grotto.

1.2 Arrive back at the trailhead.

15 Hocking Hills State Park: Old Man's Cave

Hike along a sandstone gorge past waterfalls, rocks, and caves to discover the mystery of Hocking Hills' hermit. Stop to see the unique streambed formation of Devil's Bathtub and view the Sphinx Head rock formation.

Distance: 1.1-mile loop with options

Approximate hiking time: 1.5 hours

Difficulty: Moderate due to slippery rock formations and rough terrain

Trail surface: Paved and rock

Best season: April through January

Other trail users: Tourists and long-distance hikers

Canine compatibility: Leashed dogs permitted

Schedule: Dawn until dusk year-round except in mid-January, when the park closes to the public for an annual winter hike from 9:00 a.m. until noon

Maps: USGS Logan; Hocking Hills and Old Man's Cave maps, available for download at www .dnr.state.oh.us

Trail contacts: Hocking Hills State Park, 19852 Route 664 South, Logan, OH 43138; (740) 385-6842; www.dnr.state.oh .us/parks/parks/hocking/ tabid/743/Default.aspx

Finding the trailhead: From U.S. Highway 33 South, take the exit for Route 664 South. Drive 11 miles and turn left into the parking lot near the Old Man's Cave Visitor Center. Trailheads are located directly next to the center. GPS coordinates: N26 04.80' / W82 32.47'

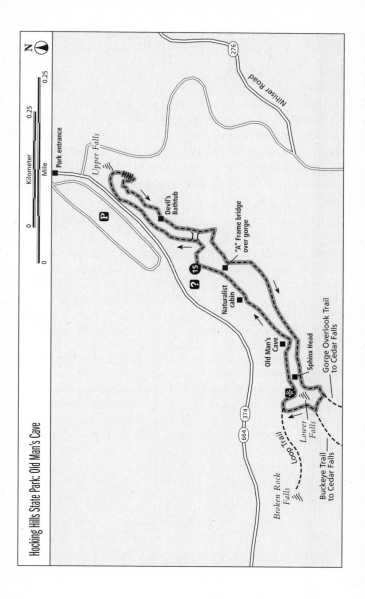

Hocking Hills State Park: Old Man's Cave

The Hike

This 1.1-mile loop hike in Hocking Hills State Park features spectacular terrain as it winds past waterfalls, ominous caves, elaborate rock formations, and hemlock-lined trails. Nestled in this wooded park 56 miles from Columbus, Old Man's Cave is the most popular natural attraction in the area, drawing hiking enthusiasts, families, and tourists year-round.

Some of the earliest inhabitants of the Hocking Hills region arrived in the mid-1700s and included the Wyandot, Delaware, and Shawnee Indians. Their name for the Hocking River was "Hockhocking," or "bottle river," for its surrounding bottle-shaped valley. The weathering and erosion of the ancient blackhand sandstone and shale have formed most of the recess caves surrounding Old Man's Cave.

The trails surrounding Old Man's Cave are relatively short, but the gorge actually extends for nearly 1.5 miles and is 150 feet at its deepest point. In addition to hemlock, black birch and Canada yew can be found nestled inside the gorge.

Folklore surrounding Old Man's Cave focuses on a hermit named Richard Rowe, who lived in the area around 1796. He traveled from the Cumberland Mountains of Tennessee to establish a trading post and discovered the Hocking Hills region while looking for game. It's believed he accidentally killed himself with his own gun and local Indians buried him beneath a recess or near a cave. Part of the challenge of this hike is guessing where he's buried.

Other white settlers in the area were brothers Nathaniel and Pat Rayon, who settled in 1795 and built a cabin near Old Man's Cave. They're also thought to be buried in a cave or somewhere nearby. Their cabin was eventually relocated to the nearby Iles farm and used as a tobacco-drying house.

By 1870 the cave areas of Hocking Hills were already considered scenic attractions, and in 1924 the state of Ohio made its first land purchase in an effort to preserve the area's beauty. Old Man's Cave was included in that parcel, and by the 1970s cottages, cabins, and campgrounds had begun springing up in the region.

Start your hike at the trailhead adjacent to the left of the visitor center and walk northwest along the rim of Old Man's Gorge. As you gain ground on your hike, you'll notice that Old Man's Creek divides the sandstone gorge. It's easy to explore rims, ridges, and rock formations without straying too far off the main trail below.

At 0.2 mile walk over the Upper Falls area. From here you can walk down the adjacent staircase to the falls and stand on the banks to get a majestic view of the falls from below.

Continue walking south and cross Old Man's Creek to view the Devil's Bathtub at 0.4 mile. The swirling water and bubbling froth along this unique streambed is a pothole in a weakened layer of the blackhand sandstone that has widened over time. Legend has it that the pothole extends all the way down to Hades.

At 0.6 mile look for a series of tunnels and rocky stairs opening up to a gorge leading to the cave. In 1930 the Works Progress Administration (WPA) created the trails, stone stairs, and tunnels that snake around Old Man's Cave, making for a spectacular hike. The cave itself is 200 feet long, 50 feet high, and 75 feet deep. This might just be the spot where the old hermit is buried.

Continue downstream and make your way to the Lower Falls. The 40-foot lower falls are lined with majestic sandstone walls and peppered with hemlocks and ferns. Spring wildflowers are abundant and include trilliums, Dutchman's breeches, trout lilies, violets, and wild columbines. At 0.9 mile you'll see the Sphinx Head rock formation.

Continue back to the trailhead. This loop is ideal for hikers who want to see both sides of the valley floor and explore rock formations and crevices. Although spring through fall is your best bet for a leisurely day hike on mostly dry terrain, an annual winter hike in January draws adventurous novice and expert hikers each year. Frozen waterfalls and fresh snowfalls give the region a stunning winter landscape.

Old Man's Cave is also part of the Grandma Gatewood Trail, named for the famous Ohio hiker Emma Gatewood. At the tender age of sixty-seven, Gatewood decided to hike the entire Appalachian Trail after reading that no woman had ever hiked its entirety. She hiked the AT several times during her lifetime (in her tennis shoes), but her favorite trail was the 6.0-mile stretch that connects Old Man's Cave, Cedar Falls, and Ash Cave and is now known as Grandma Gatewood Trail. She also led the first winter hike in the park and continued to do so for more than a decade.

While the Old Man's Cave hike is an easy enough excursion for kids and dogs, the 1.1-mile hike will take upwards of an hour and a half due to rocky terrain and the dense crowds that gather during summer months. For hikers looking for something more strenuous, a variety of easy to difficult trails extend throughout the park system. Continuing south from Old Man's Cave will take you to Ash Cave for a 10.0-mile out-and-back hike.

Keep children close and dogs on-leash at all times, especially if you plan to explore adjacent trails leading to overlooks and potentially slippery ridges. Although a popular hiking destination in winter, the paths are slick and can be dangerous without proper precautions. Hiking boots with adequate traction are recommended year-round.

Miles and Directions

0.0 Start at Old Man's Cave Visitor Center and turn left onto the trail.

0.2 Round the top of the Upper Falls and walk down the stairs.

0.3 Stop at the creekbank to view the falls from below.

0.4 View the Devil's Bathtub, and access bridges and stairs.

0.5 Cross bridges and climb stairs.

0.6 Come to a series of tunnels and rock stairs and continue to Old Man's Cave.

0.8 View Lower Falls.

0.9 View the Sphinx Head.

1.0 Return to trailhead.

1.1 Arrive back at the visitor center.

16 Dawes Arboretum

Hike through rolling meadows and make a loop through an ornate Japanese garden, conifers, and wooded forests. Stop by the lake and take a walk through a deciduous cypress garden.

Distance: 2.8-mile loop with options
Approximate hiking time: 2.5 hours
Difficulty: Easy
Trail surface: Grass, mulch, cement, and gravel paths
Best season: mid-April through mid-October
Other trail users: None
Canine compatibility: Leashed

dogs permitted
Schedule: Open dawn until dusk year-round except Thanksgiving, Christmas, New Year's Day, and during threatening weather
Maps: USGS quad: Thornville
Trail contacts: Dawes Arboretum, 7770 Jacksontown Road, Newark, OH 43056; (800) 44-DAWES (32937); www.dawes arb.org

Finding the trailhead: From Columbus take Interstate 70 east for 30 miles. Turn north at exit 132 onto Route 13 and drive 2.6 miles to the Dawes Arboretum entrance on your left. Continue straight and park in the visitor center parking lot. GPS coordinates: N58 48.14' / W82 24.82'

The Hike

Nature enthusiasts Beman and Bertie Dawes founded Dawes Arboretum in 1929. Beman originally worked in the lumber industry and developed an intense passion for trees. His wife was a self-taught naturalist, and they combined their knowledge of trees and gardening to create the arbo–

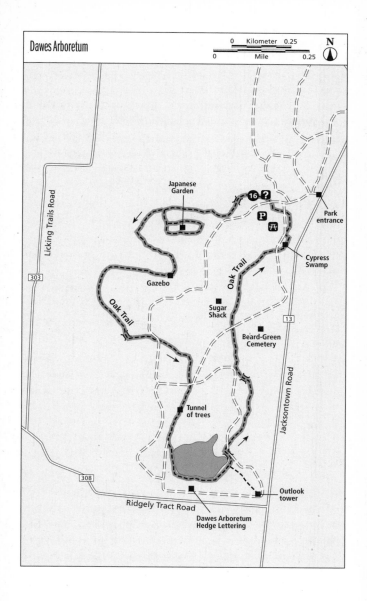

retum. His brother, Charles Dawes, was the vice president while Calvin Coolidge was in office and was also winner of the Nobel Peace Prize. Charles assisted in the endowment to fund the arboretum.

Today Dawes Arboretum includes upwards of 1,800 acres and 8 miles of hiking trails featuring more than 15,000 plants, a Japanese garden, an azalea glen, an all-seasons garden, Ohio buckeyes, a conifer glen, a bonsai garden, a cypress swamp, and a museum.

The Daweswood House Museum was once home to a local farmer and blacksmith named John Brumback, who built the house between 1866 and 1867. The Dawes family bought the Brumback home and 140 acres of land. Visitors can see nineteenth- and twentieth-century antiques and memorabilia from the Dawes homes.

Beman Dawes also developed the tree dedication program at the arboretum, and since 1927 more than one hundred trees have been dedicated to various groups and individuals. The park continues to conserve the natural habitats of the park with a focus on restoring or re-creating the state's native ecosystems, including its wetlands and grasslands. The arboretum's rich diversity makes for a leisurely place to spend the day walking the trails, visiting the museum, and lounging by the lake.

Start your hike to the left of the visitor center by picking up Oak Trail. Unlike most of the hikes at surrounding state and metro parks, the arboretum trails are identified with markers and signage to explain the surrounding trees and vegetation. As you wind past the parking lots and into the meadow, look for serviceberry, shagbark hickory, black walnut, and maples.

At about 0.3 mile bear left for the Japanese Garden

Trail. The short loop is well worth the effort and houses a small pond, shrubbery, ornamental rocks, and raked sand. Designed in 1963 by landscape architect and University of Kyoto lecturer Dr. Makoto Nakamura, the gardens were built as a complement to the bonsai collection on display in front of the visitor center. Walk on the stepping-stones across the pond and past the meditation house on your way back to Oak Trail at 0.6 mile.

The trail slopes upward through the forest past wild sunflowers, echinacea, and a small gazebo. Inside, you'll see the trailhead sign for Holly Trail pointing to your left and Oak Trail on the right. Keep right and explore the deciduous hollies and an impressive black maple along the park's rolling hills. This region of the park doesn't offer much canopy coverage, so bring a hat and sunscreen on a sunny day.

Continue walking beneath the canopy of trees and make your way to Dawes Lake. As you loop around the tranquil water, you will be treated to the sight of some 2,000 feet of hedge lettering, spelling out DAWES ARBORETUM. Just beyond the hedges and the lake, an observation tower affords an overview of the shrub lettering and park.

On the return trip, walk over the short wooden bridges and boardwalks as the path enters Conifer Glen, which features fourteen acres of conifers ranging from compact to full size.

At 2.3 miles note the small cemetery on your right and shortly thereafter a log cabin on your left. The cemetery is the final resting place of the Beard-Green family, the first legal settlers in Licking County. A nearby sign details information about the dates and family tree of the family's descendants. The cabin was once used for making maple syrup. It's still a working sugar shack, and educational programs and tours demonstrate how maple syrup is made. You won't see the entire process—it takes nearly eight hours to boil down forty gallons of sugar maple sap into just one gallon of syrup.

When you reach 2.6 miles, loop through the short trail in the Cypress Swamp garden. This is the northernmost bald cypress swamp in North America, and visitors can walk along its boardwalk to see the swampy terrain up close. The surrounding vernal pools house northern water snakes, frogs, dragonflies, and during winter through spring, Jefferson and spotted salamanders.

While you're here, take a moment to read more about the deciduous tree's "knees," which grow from the roots and peer up through the murky water. Scientists aren't exactly sure what purpose the knees serve, but it's thought they help bring oxygen to the submerged roots and protect the trees from high winds and unstable environments.

When you exit the Cypress Swamp, continue walking and turn right to make your way back to the visitor center and parking lot. You can also access the 5.0-mile East Trail from the Cypress Swamp through a prairie ecosystem, beech-maple forest, and Adena mound. Ask for a free permit and map at the visitor center.

Before you leave the arboretum you might want to pay a visit to the five wetland ponds at the park's Dutch Fork Wetlands area. This section of the park is home to seasonal migrating and nesting birds. Guided tours of the grounds, including auto tours, are also available through the visitor center.

Miles and Directions

0.0 Start at Dawes Arboretum Visitor Center and pick up the Oak Trail.

0.3 Bear left for the Japanese garden loop.

0.6 End the Japanese garden loop and return to the Oak Trail.

1.6 Walk through tunnel of trees to Dawes Lake.

1.8 Look for hedge lettering at the southeast end of the lake.

2.3 Pass the Beard-Green cemetery.

2.4 Walk past the sugar shack.

2.6 Walk through Cypress Swamp.

2.8 Arrive back at the visitor center.

17 Blackhand Gorge State Nature Preserve

Walk along the rim of a sandstone gorge cut by the Licking River. Learn more about the park's mysterious Native American legacy and ancient namesake. Hikers are rewarded with views of a quarry from the 1800s, towering cliffs, jagged rock, and sandstone outcroppings.

Distance: 1.8-mile loop

Approximate hiking time: 1.5 hours

Difficulty: Easy, with a well worn trail and partially paved trail system

Trail surface: Paved, rock, and dirt

Best season: March through November

Other trail users: Bicyclists and runners

Canine compatibility: Leashed dogs permitted on paved Blackhand Trail only

Schedule: Daily from a half hour before sunrise to a half hour after sunset

Maps: USGS Thornville

Contacts: Blackhand Gorge State Nature Preserve, 2045 Morse Road, Building F-1, Columbus, OH 43229-6693; (740) 763-4411; www.dnr.state .oh.us/tabid/922/default.aspx

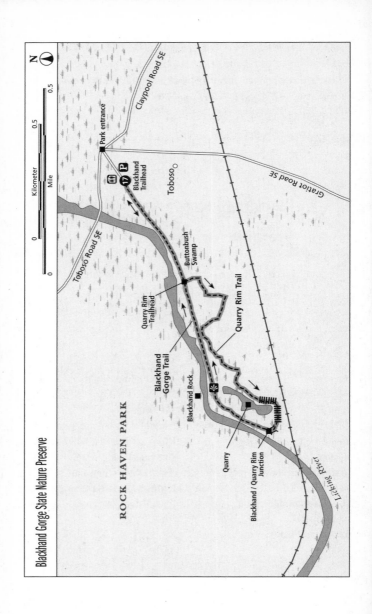

Blackhand Gorge State Nature Preserve

Finding the trailhead: From Interstate 70 in Zanesville take Route 146 west for 17 miles. Exit at County Road 273, marked with a sign for Toboso and Blackhand Gorge State Nature Preserve. Turn left and drive 1.8 miles to the small parking lot on the right next to the restrooms. GPS coordinates: N3 21.49' / W82 13.10'

The Hike

Blackhand Gorge was named for a mysterious ancient petroglyph, or rock drawing, of a large hand impression on its wall. Legend has it that the soot-colored hand marked the boundary of a sacred Native American territory where no man was to raise his hand against another. Another story says it was a directional sign to the flint deposits in neighboring Flint Ridge. It's thought that the region beyond the black hand and around Flint Ridge provided neutral territory for tribes looking for the valuable flint. The hand was destroyed when workers dynamited the walls of the cliff during construction of the Ohio-Erie Canal towpath in the 1800s, but the name of the gorge stuck.

The gorge also has a long history of providing transportation to settlers over the centuries. Native American and European explorers once used the route where the river cuts an east–west gorge. In the 1820s construction for the Ohio and Erie Canal was erected along the now-dry Canal Lock Trail on the river's north side. In the twentieth century the gorge was blasted to build a tunnel for a trolley route. Visitors won't be able to access the tunnel—it lies on private property—but you can still see a newer elevated rail line running over the gorge.

In 1975 Blackhand Gorge was dedicated as an interpretive nature preserve to ensure its aesthetic, scientific, and educational values are preserved for the public. For hikers, the 981-acre preserve features waterside, rock ledge, and wooded trails in addition to a paved 4.0-mile path for cyclists and visitors with dogs. The paved trail is also one of the few wheelchair-accessible trails in the region and is currently the only bike trail in the Ohio preserve system.

Start the loop hike at the parking lot on the east end of the preserve on the paved Blackhand Gorge Trail. Note the small overlook spur on your left, which offers views of a buttonbush swamp and the plant's round flowers at 0.3 mile as you walk along the water. At 0.4 mile turn left for the Quarry Rim Trail to hike around the rim of the sandstone quarry that operated from the 1870s until the 1920s. The quarry is now filled with water.

Hikers accessing the Quarry Rim Trail will be rewarded with overlook views of rugged walls, towering cliffs, and jagged outcroppings from exposed conglomeratic sandstone. It's also a great way to see a variety of vegetation, whether from the rim or while looking down below. Scan the floodplains and try to spot the sycamore, cottonwood, and box elder. Hemlocks and yellow and cherry birch can be found on the north side of the gorge.

Along the drier region in the hills of the gorge, oak, Virginia pine, hickory, and mountain laurel can be found. Regardless of the trail, the preserve is peppered with such wildflowers as Solomon's seal, phlox, and trillium during spring. Year-round, white-tailed deer can also be found looking for a treat among the forest litter.

After looking out over the preserve, carefully look down into the gorge. Hardwoods and spring flora can be found clustering around the slopes and ravines. The gorge is about 320 feet at its deepest point, with plenty of makeshift overlook points from the surrounding rock. Look around for the thick roots of yellow birch trees and other hardwoods spilling out across the sandstone and making small steps throughout the trail. The unique pattern of fingers across rock lends to the legacy of the black hand once engraved in the gorge.

When you complete the Quarry Rim Trail, turn right at 1.0 mile and pick up the paved multiuse trail you started on. While the rim offers spectacular views, walking through the "Deep Cut" blasted out by the Central Ohio Railroad in the 1850s is an unmatched experience. The Deep Cut, which took around 1,200 kegs of gunpowder to create, runs 330 feet long, 65 feet deep, and 30 feet wide. Construction of the cut lent to the towering rock walls lining the path.

On the way back to the parking lot, pick up the Black-hand Stone Spur Trail at 1.2 miles to see the river's edge and 100 feet of sandstone outcroppings and towering cliffs. Notice the sandstone block walls that were once a part of the Ohio and Erie Canal towpath. If you have a pair of binoculars, look around for pileated woodpeckers, yellow-crowned kinglets, Carolina chickadees, and tufted titmice in the trees nearby. Some hikers have reportedly seen a few elusive bald eagles in the area.

If you're looking for more hiking at Blackhand Gorge, access the 2.3-mile Chestnut Trail west of the Blackhand Trail. This spur on the south side of the river leads to the end of the multiuse path and makes for a 10.0-mile round-trip walk. The Marie Hickey and Oak Knob loop is a less-crowded hike along the north side of the gorge. Although rock climbing is prohibited, visitors can canoe and fish in the preserve.

Miles and Directions

0.0 Start at trailhead off the parking lot and restrooms.

0.3 Look for the buttonbush swamp.

0.4 Turn left onto the Quarry Rim Trail.

0.7 Look over the gorge rim for views of the river and the paved path below.

1.0 Turn right onto the Blackhand Gorge Trail.

1.2 Pick up the Blackhand Stone Spur Trail to access the overlook.

1.4 Go straight at the junction to remain on the Blackhand Gorge Trail.

1.8 Arrive back at the trailhead.

About the Author

Susan Finch is a freelance writer and hiker who special-
izes in budget, family, and recreational travel. Her work
has appeared in national outlets, and she travels regularly
throughout North America and Europe. When she's not
writing and traveling from her home in the New York City
region, Susan and her husband, Drew, are planning their
next trip, hiking, or spending time off in his home state of
Ohio.